MIND
POWER

MIND POWER

ESP and Other Psychic Mysteries

SANDRA COLLIER

Cover by
Thomas Dannenberg

Scholastic Canada Ltd.

Scholastic Canada Ltd.
175 Hillmount Road, Markham, Ontario L6C 1Z7

Scholastic Inc.
555 Broadway, New York, NY 10012, USA

Scholastic Australia Pty Limited
PO Box 579, Gosford, NSW 2250, Australia

Scholastic New Zealand Limited
Private Bag 94407, Greenmount,
Auckland, New Zealand

Scholastic Ltd.
Villiers House, Clarendon Avenue, Leamington Spa,
Warwickshire CV32 5PR, UK

Design by: Andrea Casault

Canadian Cataloguing in Publication Data

Collier, Sandra
  Mind power

ISBN 0-590-03835-4

1. Parapsychology — Juvenile literature. I. Title.

BF1031.C644 1998   j133.8   C98-930949-5

  6 5 4 3 2 1   Printed in Canada   8 9/9 0 1 2 3 4 /0

For
Alexander, Sidney and Tobin.

I am indebted to Sheila Ostrander and Lynn Schroeder, authors of *Psychic Discoveries,* and to Arthur Lyons and Marcello Truzzi Ph.D., authors of *The Blue Sense.* These two excellent books provided much of the source material for the chapters on crime and psychic espionage.

Also, heartfelt thanks to Joanne Richter, Sandy Bogart Johnston and Rosemary Toth for their guidance and skill, and appreciation to the redoubtable Kerner Express.

Contents

Introduction

Like most people, there were things I just "knew" without knowing how I knew them. I had hunches about things. But I didn't believe in ESP or psychic powers. Everything I couldn't explain I called coincidence. Frankly, I thought ESP was a lot of nonsense.

But then something happened that made me question everything I had previously believed. The following story may sound unbelievable but I swear that it's true:

I have worked as a dream therapist for many years. One day a client told me a dream he'd had the night before. He dreamed that my son (whom he'd never seen) had jumped over a fence and fallen, hurting himself very badly. Before I could open my mouth to ask him about his dream, there was a loud rapping at my door. My secretary called out, "Sandra, there's been an accident! Your son's in the hospital!"

I rushed to the hospital and learned that my son had jumped over a chain that was hanging across the school driveway. His foot had caught on the chain, and he had fallen, hard. He'd suffered serious internal injuries.

I was shaken by my client's dream, but I told myself that it was a coincidence. After all, there's no way anyone could know something before it really happened.

Then, a few weeks later, that very same man told me about another dream. This time it was about my daughter! I felt anxious as he told me about it. He'd dreamed that my daughter had an accident at school and that she'd hurt her head. Unbelievably, I heard the same knock on my door, and the same urgent message: "Your daughter's had an accident! She's at the hospital!"

My daughter had been playing baseball at her school. A fly ball had hit her and split open her forehead. She needed several stitches, and you can still see the scar on her forehead, just above her eye, more than twenty years later.

I couldn't understand this at all. This client didn't often dream about my children. In fact, these were the only dreams he was to report about them in all the years I knew him. He didn't usually dream about accidents or injuries. What was going on?

THE MYSTERY DEEPENS

One evening about two months later, my husband and I decided to attend a conference in Hawaii. At this point, no one else knew I was planning a trip to Hawaii. The next day I went to work. As luck would have it, I saw the same man again. He came into my office and said:

I had the strangest dream last night. It makes no sense to me at all. I dreamed about a blue

and white airplane. It was flying to Hawaii
and it crashed!

When I heard this dream I got really scared. After all, he'd been right about my children. Why wouldn't he be right this time? And how strange that the very night I decided to go to Hawaii, he dreamed about Hawaii. What if *this* dream came true? Should I go or not? Should I cancel a wonderful trip because of a dream?

I tried to think clearly. There was nothing about me being on the plane in the dream. Was that important? Did that mean that I would be safe? What if I *was* in the dream and he just left that part out? Or forgot it? What to do?

This is what I did: I called my travel agent and asked her what airlines flew to Hawaii. She told me. Then I asked her, "What colours are their planes?" There was a long silence. I felt like an idiot. She told me one airline had blue and white planes, but she wasn't sure about the others.

I discovered that one company had red and white airplanes. Even though it cost more and the flights were not as convenient, I was determined I would not fly to Hawaii on a blue and white plane!

I have never been as frightened as I was on that flight to Hawaii. But we landed safely, to my huge relief. We collected our bags and got into a taxi. The driver turned in his seat and said, "It'll be a while folks. There's been a plane crash."

My heart was in my mouth as I whispered, "Do you know what colour the plane was?"

"Sure do, ma'am," he replied. "It was blue and white."

I was deeply shaken. I could no longer dismiss these events as coincidence and I resolved to find an explanation. I began to research and explore everything I could find about ESP.

I learned that there is a lot of misunderstanding and confusion about ESP. Sometimes people exaggerate their experiences. Sometimes a true experience becomes more and more embellished as it is told and retold. And sometimes there is even downright fraud and trickery.

To my surprise, as I sorted my way through the confusion and hype, I discovered that there is a vast amount of real, factual and documented information about ESP and other psychic experiences. Does this information prove the existence of ESP? Read on, consider the evidence and then be the judge!

CHAPTER 1

The Mystery of Psychic Perception

Have you ever met a stranger and felt a kind of "click," an instant liking towards that person? Have you ever disliked someone for no apparent reason? Sometimes people call this kind of reaction "chemistry." But this so-called chemistry could more correctly be called psychic perception. You are picking up, or sensing, information that is available to you outside the realm of your physical senses.

You can experience psychic perception in many different ways. Michelle, who's sixteen, told me the following:

> *I sometimes see things happen before they actually occur. My grandmother told me I had "the sight," and that it was a gift. When I've tried to talk to my friends about it, they think I'm crazy. My father told me I have too much*

imagination, so now I don't talk about it. But I still have it. It's not something I can just shut off like a tap. Sometimes it's there and sometimes it isn't. I don't seem to have any control over it. I wish I could understand it more.

And Brad had this experience:

One night I woke up in a cold sweat. My twin brother was calling my name, except he wasn't in the house, he was in Nicaragua, working with a relief agency. I was certain he was in trouble, that he needed help, but it was the middle of the night, and there was no way I could reach him. Two days later we heard that his compound had been attacked and my brother was wounded at the same time I heard him calling me!

You may have had similar experiences yourself. Perhaps you have thought of someone you haven't seen in a long time and that person called you the same day. Or maybe sometimes you just *know* what your friend is thinking before he or she even begins to speak. You might have been to see a psychic or a fortuneteller who told you things about you and your family that no one else could possibly know.

All these experiences are part of a phenomenon called extrasensory perception, or ESP. There is enormous interest in ESP and other psychic experiences. In fact, studies show that anywhere from fifty to eighty percent of the population claims to have had one or more psychic experiences. Rob, who's eighteen, told me:

> *Ever since I can remember, I've seen things that*
> *other people can't see. At first I just assumed*
> *everyone else could see them too. But one day,*
> *when I was about five or six, I told my mother*
> *that there was a lady in a red dress in the*
> *kitchen. My mother couldn't see her. When I*
> *insisted that there really was a lady there, she*
> *told me, "Robert, we are Scottish, we don't see*
> *such things." After that, I kept quiet. But I still*
> *see them. They look like regular people except*
> *they're kind of transparent. I can see through them.*

What exactly is ESP? There is a lot of confusion about psychic experiences and ESP. Are UFOs and astrology part of ESP? What about crystals, faith healing and tarot cards? Is ESP the same thing as psychic phenomena? You probably have other questions as well. Or you might be understandably skeptical, like Stephanie. She related this experience:

> *A psychic told me that someone in my family*
> *would develop a health problem very soon. I was*
> *really worried that my father would have a heart*
> *attack. He has high blood pressure, and he's*

under a lot of pressure at work. But what
happened was that I developed eczema. My
doctor told me that it's caused by stress. Now I
wonder if I made the psychic's prediction come
true myself, like a self-fulfilling prophecy!

You might have read that the actor and comedian Chris Farley of "Saturday Night Live" fame repeatedly told his friends that he would die when he was thirty-three. Was this truly what we would call precognition (the prediction of future events), or was it something he made happen because he believed it so strongly?

Is psychic perception real? Or is it a combination of coincidence and trickery? There certainly have been many outright frauds, as you will see in Chapter 10, Fakes and Frauds. However, there are also many well-documented, apparently genuine experiences as well. Ultimately, you must be the judge.

Let's begin our exploration into the mystery of psychic perception by first of all looking at the ordinary, regular, sensory way your mind receives its information.

YOUR FIVE SENSES

Most of the information that you have about yourself and the world around you comes from your physical senses. Human beings have five physical senses: sight, sound, taste, touch and smell. Your brain receives information through one or more of these physical senses, and tells you things about the world around you.

If you're like most people, it is the information your senses bring you that determines whether you believe something is real. Many people feel that "seeing is believing."

But sometimes our senses are not totally reliable. Sometimes they can even deceive us. For example: Al, Theresa and Kim all witnessed a bank robbery on their way home from school. Al told the police that the getaway car was green. Theresa was certain the car was blue and Kim said for sure it was grey. Three different witnesses saw three different things! But here's the amazing part: That night, Al dreamed about the bank robbery. In his dream, the robbers were brothers, and the car they were driving was silver, not green, as he had first reported.

The police did catch the robbers. And wouldn't you know it? Al's psychic perception was better than his ordinary senses. It turned out that the robbers really were brothers and their car really was silver!

A SIXTH SENSE?

Al, like Michelle and Brad and many others, knows things in ways that we cannot understand or explain. Some people believe that this is because there is another sense, a sixth sense, that can pick up information that the other five senses cannot. This sixth sense is considered to be psychic.

WHAT DOES PSYCHIC MEAN?

Psyche is the Greek word for mind or consciousness. Today the word *psychic* means not physical. We use the word psychic to describe mental, subconscious or spiritual matters.

Fifteen-year-old Dana told me:

> *My mother sometimes goes to see a psychic. She*
> *has told my mother things about our family that*
> *no one else knew. She even told my mother that I*
> *was skipping school. How could she know that?*

Someone who is psychic is sensitive to non-physical forces. He or she can respond to energy that most of us are not aware of. Psychics are people who have highly developed extrasensory abilities. Professional psychics charge a fee for their services. Some may combine their psychic abilities with some other form of divination such as palm reading or tarot cards.

WHAT IS PSYCHIC ENERGY?

Psychic energy is the force, or energy, that is created by your thoughts and feelings.

Try this experiment: Look in a mirror and think of your worst teacher, the one who was always on your case. Breathe, and be aware of what happens to your body as you think about this person. Your muscles will tense and your breathing and heart rate will speed up. Just thinking about this teacher brings on a hostile, draining tension. Look closely at your mouth and eyes. Now think of the person you love most in the world. Breathe, and be aware of how your body feels as you think about this person. Again, look closely at your mouth and eyes.

Most people can see a difference in their mouths and eyes when they do this experiment, but almost everyone can feel the difference in their bodies. Your thoughts can create energy that you experience in a physical way.

Although we can all feel our own psychic energy, sometimes we can experience another person's psychic energy too. Try doing this same experiment with a friend: Focus on someone or something you feel strongly about. Ask your friend what he or she felt while you were concentrating. Then reverse roles, and see how you feel while your friend focuses on someone or something. Did either of you feel a change? If you did, you had the beginnings of a real psychic experience!

CHAPTER 2

ESP Facts

There are many different kinds of psychic experiences, but ESP is the one most people have experienced and reported. This chapter describes many of the facts that researchers have learned about ESP.

WHAT EXACTLY IS ESP ANYHOW?

ESP stands for extrasensory perception. This means perception or knowledge that comes to you outside of, or beyond, your physical senses. Perception can refer to anything from vividly "seeing" or dreaming an event to having a vague hunch or feeling, as Peggy describes:

> *I am an adopted child who found some of my maternal family ten years ago. My birth mother had died by the time I found them. One of the first things I asked was, "When did she die?"*

When I got home I looked in my journal. On that
day I had written, "I feel someone close to me
has died."

The term ESP was first used in Europe in the 1920s. In 1934, an American named J. B. Rhine began the first serious studies of ESP. Dr. Rhine divided ESP into four areas: telepathy, clairvoyance, precognition and psychokinesis.

TELEPATHY

The transfer of information from one person to another without using the five senses is called telepathy. Thoughts, feelings and emotions are communicated using only the mind. One mother described a telepathic experience with her little girl:

Rosie had crawled into bed with me in the
morning. I was thinking about some furniture
our landlady had offered to sell us. I wondered
fleetingly why the woman didn't like children.
Just then Rosie asked, "Why doesn't she like
children?" Surprised, I asked, "What made you
think of her?" Rosie answered, "Oh, I was just
thinking about her furniture."

Telepathy usually happens between two people who know each other well. The stronger the emotional bond, the more likely telepathy will occur. This bond can be either positive or negative.

13

You could be telepathic with someone you really dislike! Telepathy can take place in both waking and dream states.

When Sue was eleven, she had this telepathic experience:

> We were doing Social Studies at school when all of a sudden I got this terrible pain in my chest. I heard my mother crying. She was calling my name. I just knew something terrible had happened. When I got home my aunt told me that the roof on one of the big stores downtown had collapsed. It was full of shoppers and my mom was one of them. She was in hospital, but she was OK. Some people died. My mom was one of the lucky survivors. But I had heard her calling me!

Here's another example of a telepathic experience: When Napoleon was exiled on the island of Elba, he met daily with his staff. One day, while speaking to his generals, he suddenly and for no apparent reason began to cry. He later discovered that at that very moment, Josephine, his first wife and great love, was dying at her home outside Paris.

CLAIRVOYANCE

The word clairvoyance literally means clear seeing, but in reality it means having mental impressions about people or events. People often confuse clairvoyance and telepathy but the differ-

14

ence is really very simple. Telepathy is about *mental* states — it is mind-to-mind communication. Clairvoyance is about *objects* or *events* — it often involves visions of events at a distance in space or time.

Although clairvoyant impressions are usually vague and fuzzy, they can sometimes be startlingly accurate. In his book *Extraordinary Experiences*, John Robert Colombo tells of a deep-sea diver who drowned in Lake Memphremagog in Quebec. Many attempts were made to recover the body, including the use of a miniature submarine. But because the lake is so deep, all attempts were unsuccessful. A clairvoyant from Alexandria, Ontario, made an exact drawing of where the body would be found. He said it was lying at a depth of 70 metres of water at the foot of a cliff 180 metres from shore. The body would be lying on its back with its feet on the cliff, and the diving suit would have red spots on it. A diver followed the clairvoyant's directions and found the body precisely as he had predicted. Instead of red spots, however, the drowned man's diving suit had red stripes!

The most common form of clairvoyance occurs when someone dying or in crisis appears in a vision to a loved one. This vision can be experienced as a ghost or, as this family experienced, a disembodied voice:

I heard my brother, who was stationed in France during World War II, call my name. I ran to the door. My father was on the porch and he saw Ken come up the walk, smiling, fully dressed in

15

> *his uniform. But when Dad extended his hand,*
> *my brother faded away, and Dad said he knew*
> *then that Ken was dead. We heard later that Ken*
> *had died at the time we saw him on the porch.*

People who have clairvoyant experiences do not have them all the time. Some may only have one or two experiences in an entire lifetime. Others, like Michelle in Chapter 1, have them more frequently.

PRECOGNITION

Both telepathy and clairvoyance operate in present time. Information is transmitted about what is happening at that moment. But precognition means knowing about an event or experience before it happens. Precognition can be either telepathic or clairvoyant.

Alice Fortune, a young woman from Winnipeg, Manitoba, was travelling in Europe with her family. The family spent a few days in Cairo, and Alice had her fortune told by a young man there. This was his prediction:

> *You are in danger every time you travel on the*
> *sea. I see you adrift in an open boat. You will*
> *lose everything but your life. You will be saved*
> *but others will be lost.*

Two months later, Alice and her family set sail on the *Titanic* for their return trip home. Alice's father and her brother lost their own lives, but they were able to get Alice into the last lifeboat before the ship went down.

A second documented case of precognition also connected the *Titanic* and a Winnipeg resident, the Reverend Charles Morgan, minister of Rosedale Methodist Church. After preparing his Sunday evening service, Rev. Morgan took a short nap. He had a kind of dream, or vision, of rushing water, with sounds and cries for help. He heard the hymn, "Hearing, Father, while we pray to Thee, for those in peril on the sea."

The vision was so upsetting to Rev. Morgan that he told his congregation about it. He asked them to sing the hymn he had heard in his vision.

The next morning the world learned that the *Titanic* had sunk. It also learned that just before the ship struck the iceberg, many of the passengers were attending a shipboard service. The hymn that was sung was, "Hearing, Father, while we pray to Thee, for those in peril on the sea."

Fortunately, not all precognitions are tragic! Sasha, a young woman in her last year of high school, had a precognitive experience that actually improved her grades. This is how Sasha described it:

> *I was doing so poorly in French that I was*
> *thinking of dropping it. One night I dreamed that*
> *my French teacher was making up a surprise*
> *test. As clear as day, I could see every question*
> *and the correct answers. The next morning I was*

> *totally amazed when my French teacher gave us*
> *a surprise test. I was even more amazed when I*
> *saw that the questions were the same as those in*
> *my dream. I remembered the answers from my*
> *dream, and I got my very first 100 on a test!*

Some people say that precognition has saved their lives. Several people who had booked passage on the ship *Titanic* were so uneasy about the voyage that they cancelled their tickets at the last minute. Colin Macdonald, a marine engineer who had made several transatlantic crossings, was offered the position of second engineer on the *Titanic* three times. Three times he turned it down, even though it would have meant a promotion for him. He said he just had a hunch that he should not sail on the *Titanic*. The man who took the job instead went down with the ship.

Aniela Jaffe, a colleague of analyst Dr. Carl Jung, has collected many other stories. She tells of a mother who cancelled her seven-year-old son's school trip because she had a sudden premonition of danger. That night, there was a terrible train crash. The wrecked train was the very one that the boy and his mother would have travelled on.

Canadian writer Sidney Katz has also documented some cases of precognition. One case he described took place in British Columbia. A man who was booked on a flight to Vancouver had a sudden, overwhelming conviction that the plane was going to crash. Even though he was already in his seat, the feeling was so strong that the man got up and left the plane. The plane took off without the man, and crashed into the side of Mt. Benson.

Unfortunately, the only way we can tell if a precognition is genuine is after the fact. After all, many feelings of premonition do not come true. However, it is possible that these feelings serve as warnings, which, if heeded, would then change a likely outcome.

In the 1960s, a U.S. mathematician named William Cox researched trains that had crashed or derailed. He discovered that the trains travelling on the day of the accident carried significantly fewer passengers than trains travelling before or after the day of the crash. Also, in every case, there were fewer passengers travelling in the damaged coaches than usual. Cox believes that many people switch their travel plans without realizing they are responding to a precognitive warning.

There are now several agencies that collect information on precognition. It has been found that these agencies receive an increase of reports just prior to major disasters, although few of the descriptions accurately predict the actual disaster. For example, the British Premonitions Bureau, located in London, England, received a report that a number of young children would panic, rush to the end of a room, and die there. Four days later, in Beauvais, France, fourteen children died in a school fire.

The British Premonitions Bureau was founded after a terrible disaster occurred in Wales. On October 21, 1966, an avalanche of coal slammed into a school, killing 128 children. In all, 144 people were killed in the tragedy. Over 200 people claimed foresight, and many had dreamed about it. Several of these precognitive dreams were recorded in writing before the disaster occurred.

Psychiatrist Dr. John Barker researched these premonitions and identified sixty which he thought were genuine. He was so convinced by these premonitions that he became a founding member of the Bureau in 1967.

There are two registries in the United States that collect premonitions as part of an ongoing research project. They are the Central Premonitions Registry in New York City and the Premonitions Registry Bureau located in Berkeley, California. Although most of the reported premonitions do not seem to come true, some have been startlingly accurate. What is even more interesting is that the New York registry has learned that the same five people have reported nearly half of all the accurate predictions!

PSYCHOKINESIS

Psychokinesis, or PK, comes from the Greek words for soul or mind, and motion. Today, we use the term mind over matter to describe psychokinesis. It means the ability to influence objects or things using the mind. Several years ago, a shocking example of psychokinesis was reported in newspapers across the United States and Canada:

> *In California, a teenaged girl was found walking*
> *down a country road. Her arms had been*
> *chopped off by a deranged man an hour earlier.*
> *Over and over she mumbled, "I'm the Bionic*
> *Woman."*

It is astounding that, an hour after the attack, the girl had not collapsed or died from loss of blood. The teen explained later that what she was actually doing was trying to stop herself from bleeding to death. She held the image of the television character in her mind, imagining that she was a machine and therefore couldn't bleed.

Psychokinesis is the most controversial aspect of ESP. It usually refers to the moving or changing of objects by using the mind — bending metal, for example. It can also refer to feats such as levitation. There have been reports that some saints and other spiritual masters have been able to overcome the force of gravity to levitate.

In the sixteenth century, Saint Theresa of Avila was observed to rise into the air while she was praying. Saint Joseph of Copertino, a seventeenth-century Franciscan monk, was also observed to levitate. Of course, it is impossible to verify these reports.

Russian scientists claim that a woman called Nina Kulagina could move objects by concentrating on them. She has been observed moving non-magnetic objects a short distance, even when the objects were placed under glass.

During a PK session, Kulagina's heart rate rose to 240 beats per minute. She would lose more than a kilogram of body weight, and there were measurable changes to her blood sugar, brain waves and endocrine system. Afterwards, she was left with pain, weakness and no sense of taste.

Kulagina was tested and studied by Russian scientists for thirty years, until her death in 1990. Western scientists, however, were able to observe her feats only in Soviet laboratories — they were not allowed to conduct their own tests. For this reason, researchers cannot rule out the possibility that Kulagina might have used trickery during her tests.

Robert Jahn, Dean of Engineering at Princeton University in New Jersey, designs testing machines for ESP experiments. He became interested in ESP when he discovered, unaccountably, that he was able to raise the temperature of a testing device simply by concentrating on it.

Using PK to influence inanimate objects remains controversial. It is a fact, though, that your mind can and does affect *living* matter. You can make someone feel uncomfortable just by being in a bad mood. Tony, who is seventeen, told me:

> *When my sister's in a bad mood, she doesn't*
> *have to say a word! I don't even have to look at*
> *her, I can just feel it. I want to get as far away*
> *from her as I can!*

Your thoughts influence your body every minute of every day. Tests have repeatedly shown that emotions such as depression, grief, fear and rage can change the body's chemistry, which may then lead to the development of illness such as high blood pressure and ulcers. And positive thoughts and feelings like love and pleasure can bring about or speed healing. You will learn more about PK and the body in Chapter 5, Psychic Healing.

ESP AND PSI

Parapsychologists often find it difficult to know which of the four processes is occurring — telepathy, clairvoyance, precognition or psychokinesis. For example, if a psychic tells you something about your family, is she seeing this through clairvoyance or is she looking into your mind and reading your thoughts via telepathy?

In order to avoid some of this confusion, many researchers refer to ESP and other psychic phenomena as simply *psi*.

A FEW MORE FACTS

By studying ESP under laboratory conditions, researchers have been able to make observations and reach some conclusions about ESP. The following are some of the discoveries research has made.

ESP AND CHILDREN

Many parents will agree that their children have a high degree of ESP. Kelly's mother related a typical experience:

> *I opened my dresser drawer and saw Kelly's toy
> whistle. I thought to myself, "I won't mention it
> because I don't want it being blown in the
> house." Right after I thought this, Kelly asked,
> "Mommy, where is my whistle?"*

Not only do kids have ESP, they have more of it than adults! Kids, however, start losing touch with their ESP around age seven.

By the age of twelve, they have lost most of it.

Some cultures recognize and value the natural ESP of children. In the former Abyssinia, authorities regularly used children under twelve years of age as thief catchers. These children were reportedly able to track down thieves and murderers using their ESP.

But you don't have to lose your psychic abilities. In Chapter 12, you can find out ways to re-awaken your sleeping ESP powers.

ESP AND TWINS

It is a popular belief that twins know each other's thoughts. But parapsychologists who have experimented with twins have not found this to be so. Although ESP does occur between twins, they do not exhibit higher ESP ratings than other strongly bonded family members.

ESP AND GENDER

Many people believe that women have more psychic ability than men, probably because many books and movies show women as fortunetellers gazing into crystal balls or reading palms. But all the studies that have been done throughout the world show that men and women are about equal in their extrasensory abilities.

ESP AND GHOSTS

ESP has nothing to do with ghosts or other supernatural phenomena. Supernatural events, such as miracles or interventions by a spirit or deity, lie outside the laws of nature. ESP and other forms of psi are paranormal phenomena. They are processes that are observable in nature but have not yet been scientifically explained.

The famous psychic Eileen Garrett believed the entities or spirits that spoke to her were really split-off parts of her own mind: information that came as if from an outside source was really coming from her subconscious. Edgar Cayce, another famous psychic, also said that his information came from his own or his subjects' subconscious minds.

Ghosts, astrology and UFOs are not ESP. Neither are crystals, tarot cards, runes, palm reading, tea-leaf reading or other means of divination. But many practictioners do use ESP in addition to these things. So, although astrology is not part of ESP, an astrologer may use his or her powers of ESP to expand or enhance an astrological reading.

ESP AND MIND READING

True mind reading is impossible because our minds hold so many different levels of awareness and thoughts at the same time. Although it is possible to telepathically transfer a predominant or highly charged thought, the full contents of your mind would be impossible to read.

CHAPTER 3

How Does ESP Work?

I was surprised to learn that many of the greatest minds in the world take ESP very seriously and try to understand it. Many respected scientists and Nobel Prize winners support the existence of psi.

Sigmund Freud thought that ESP was the original way people could understand one another before language developed. Remnants of this primitive ability may still exist deep within our brains. Under certain conditions, this ability might be triggered. According to Freud, "the transference of thoughts, the sensing of the past or the future cannot be merely accidental. If I were to live all over again, I should devote myself to psychical research rather than psychoanalysis."

Some parapsychologists have told me that ESP is accidental and cannot be explained. In their view, it's as if the universe simply hiccups occasionally. Most researchers, however, believe that ESP is not some kind of weird, unexplainable mystery. They agree with psychic Alex Tanous who said, "there is nothing supernatural about psychic experiences . . . They are quite normal. Someday, science will be able to explain the paranormal as easily as it now explains how your television set can pick up a picture."

SCIENCE AND ESP

Thanks to modern quantum physics, we have gained new ways of understanding ESP and other psi phenomena. For example, we now know that an electron has the ability to behave as either a particle *or* an energy wave. And some particles seem able to be in two places at the same time! There are subatomic particles called neutrinos that move at the speed of light and are able to pass through physical matter, like ghosts walking through walls. Some researchers told me that they believe they will soon be able to isolate substances called psi particles, or psitrons, that could transport thoughts between minds.

To these scientists, telepathy is feasible because the brain could generate psitrons that scatter and carry telepathic messages to the brains of people on the receiving end. They think that psitrons are emitted by bursts of high psychic energy, such as an intense emotional charge. These psitrons could then be absorbed by a receptive psychic system.

This process would account for the most frequently reported type of ESP experience: communication between a relaxed, often sleeping, "receiver" and a highly stressed, emotional "sender."

ESP AND VIBRATION

Every living cell in your body vibrates with energy. You are, in fact, a vibrating set of frequencies. Your brain, your eyes, your inner ears are all vibrating at many billions of cycles per second, though, of course, you are not aware of this.

The muscles in your body vibrate too, but at a low-level frequency. Even when you are deeply asleep, your body is producing vibrations. And anything that vibrates creates energy waves. This means that even when you are absolutely still and silent, you are radiating information about yourself in the form of extrasensory energy waves!

PSI WAVES?

There are different kinds of energy waves, such as sound waves and light waves. Some sense organs are more receptive to these energy waves than others. That is because cells are sensitive to different things. Some are sound sensitive, some are light sensitive and others are sensitive to heat or touch.

A snake sticks out its tongue to pick up vibrations because its tongue is more sensitive than its scaly skin. A deaf person cannot hear music through his or her ears but can still feel the vibration through touch.

You know from Chapter 1 that your thoughts can create energy. Someone who is in a bad mood can affect other people without saying a word. In the same way, a sensitive person will be affected by another person's psi waves, despite the fact that neither one is consciously aware that ESP is passing between them.

SPACE, TIME AND ESP

Most people accept the idea that ESP could pick up information in the present. But how can the mind know something that happened 100 years ago? And even more puzzling, how could it know something that hasn't even happened yet?

We do not know how the mind can transcend time and space, only that it can. The mind is capable of many extraordinary things that we cannot yet explain or understand. Consider the following example:

George and Charles are identical twins who live in New York. If asked on which date Easter will fall in 10 000 years, they will give the answer immediately. (The calculation of Easter is very difficult, because it depends on both solar and lunar cycles.)

The twins can also tell you the time of the tides on any date you ask. If you give them your date of birth, they can tell you in which years your birthday will fall on a Saturday or a Monday, or any other day of the week, for the next 40 000 years!

In another example, a six-year-old boy named Benjamin Blyth asked his father what time he was born, and instantly knew the number of seconds he had lived. His father worked the math out on paper and told the boy he was wrong by 172 800 seconds. But Ben wasn't wrong. His father had forgotten to calculate two leap years!

According to Dr. Darold Treffert, who has studied many extraordinary feats of the human mind, these children cannot explain how the answer comes, only that it comes. They do not learn the information they have; they just know it. No one understands how

29

or why this can happen. But it does happen. It is a real ability.

With ESP, the mind seems to behave in a similar fashion. It can pluck information from time and space without any conscious calculation or cognitive processing.

Wolf Messing, a famous Russian psychic, said he was able to see the future by a concentrated effort of will. "I suddenly see the final result of some event flash before me. The mechanism of direct knowledge bypasses the logical cause and effect chain and reveals to the psychic only the final link in the chain."

The air around us is teeming with invisible information which could conceivably be sensed through ESP. We are surrounded by energy waves that travel through time and space. However, most of these energy waves are outside the realm of our physical senses.

For example, if you have a dog, you know that it can hear sounds that you cannot. A homing pigeon can hear sounds with frequencies of less than one cycle per second — far too low for human ears. Low-frequency sound waves, however, can travel great distances with hardly any reduction in strength.

Some researchers think that ESP is transmitted in a similar way — through very low frequencies. Since these ultralow frequencies can travel long distances without weakening, this could explain how thoughts can be transmitted over great distances of time and space.

It is possible to experience some of these waves even though their sources no longer exist. For example, you can still see the light from stars that are dead. Although the star itself has disappeared, you can see its light waves as they travel through space.

I came across a wonderful example of the mind's ability to "time travel" when I heard a fascinating taped interview with Dr. Humphrey Osmond.

For many years, the world-renowned Dr. Osmond lived and worked in a small town in Saskatchewan, where he conducted ground-breaking research into the nature of the human mind. In one phase of his research, he used himself as a guinea pig in an experiment and described the following experience:

> *At one point I was given a sealed envelope to*
> *hold. I had a horrifying sense of absolute terror.*
> *I had a vision of a kind of Gothic mansion or*
> *castle, and the sense and smell of burning. It was*
> *truly ghastly. The experience almost wrecked me*
> *— I couldn't wait to get away from it. I was told*
> *later that the envelope contained something that*
> *came from a castle in Ireland that had burned*
> *down more than a hundred years before.*

What Dr. Osmond experienced is called psychometry. This is the ability to pick up the history of an object by holding it. The logical, scientific Osmond could hardly believe that such a thing was possible. The experience had a profound effect on him. He also described an unusual awareness of other people's thoughts, feelings and moods even though they said nothing to him. The people involved confirmed that the information Dr. Osmond's ESP was picking up was correct.

What struck Osmond most profoundly was the sense of the connectedness of all life. He saw that all things are related to each other, as if there were a kind of invisible spider's web that runs through everything.

You can read more about how to develop your own powers of psychometry in Chapter 12, Apply Your Psi.

CELLULAR ESP

Scientists know that the cells in our bodies have some way of communicating with each other. When a virus or other foreign substance penetrates your body's defence system, information instantly goes out to the rest of your body that an intruder is present. Your body immediately goes into action and tries to destroy or expel the invader. How does this communication take place? Scientists cannot fully explain it.

A fascinating experiment shows this cellular ESP most clearly: While scientists were studying living heart cells under a microscope, it was observed that an isolated single heart cell would lose its steady beating rhythm, and begin to flutter and die. However, if *two* heart cells were put close to each other (but not touching), they would begin to synchronize and beat in unison. They did not flutter and die but continued to live. The cells didn't have to touch – they could communicate across a spatial barrier.

In a similar way, people in great distress can often be calmed and comforted by the mere presence of another person. Prisoners of war have often reported that their sanity was saved by sensing that another prisoner was nearby, even though they could not communicate in any way.

ESP AND ENERGY FIELDS

The study of energy fields has also provided insights into understanding ESP. Eighteen-year-old Giselle says:

> *My boyfriend Dan has an amazing sense of direction. He can always find his way, even in a place he's never been before.*

Some people really do have a much better sense of direction than others. Scientists have found that these people are very responsive to the magnetic field that surrounds the Earth. They are able to orient themselves wherever they are, according to these magnetic fields. People like Dan just "know" where they are.

Dr. Bernard Grad has studied another type of field for more than thirty-six years. Grad, a biologist at McGill University in Montreal, studied energy fields, or bioenergy. Trained as a scientist, he conducted research into the fields of psi and energy using the highest standards of scientific methods.

As a young child, Grad had a strong awareness of being surrounded by a power, or energy, in nature. He felt he could actually see this force pulsating in the air. He remembers that at the age of four, while sitting on the grass, he could feel energy flowing into his body from the ground beneath him.

During his school years, Grad began to repress these feelings. In fact, when he was told that a doctor's bedside manner could affect his patients, Grad replied with contempt, "Believing such a thing is like believing in witchcraft!"

In university, Grad became seriously ill with tuberculosis. During the three years of his illness and recovery, he gradually rediscovered the pulsating universe he had experienced as a child. His sense of a bioenergetic connectedness to the world around him returned. While lying in bed, he could feel an ebb and flow of energy into and out of his body.

When Grad recovered, he was determined to find an explanation for his experiences. He began to read and study everything he could find that dealt with energy.

One day he happened to overhear a conversation in his laboratory. One of his technicians was talking about a psychic healer called Oskar Estebany.

Not all healers will agree to being tested, but when Grad asked if he could test Estebany's healing powers, Estebany readily agreed. For more than ten years, the two men worked together on a long succession of rigorously controlled experiments.

In addition to conducting tests with people, Grad also tested Estebany with animals, plants, water and yeasts. This was done in order to avoid all possibility of hypnotism, suggestion or other psychological influences.

Grad concluded that the biological effects observed in these experiments were caused by a force or energy released by Estebany. Grad said: "I believe the energy involved exists in a variety of different modes or frequencies . . . It can be transmitted over long distances. It doesn't depend on the 'faith' of the recipients. They need to do or believe nothing as long as they remain open or neutral."

You can read more about Oskar Estebany and his psychic abilities in Chapters 5 and 11.

ESP AND THE HUNDRETH MONKEY

In 1952, scientists were studying monkeys on the island of Koshima, off the coast of Japan. To encourage the monkeys to come closer to them, the researchers dumped sweet potatoes on the sand. The monkeys liked the taste of the sweet potatoes but they didn't like the sand and dirt that stuck to them.

One young female monkey discovered that she could clean the sand off the potatoes by washing them. She then taught her mother and some other monkeys the trick. By 1958, many of the young monkeys were washing the sandy sweet potatoes. The older monkeys kept eating the dirty potatoes.

Suddenly, the trick, which had been taught on a one-to-one basis, was common knowledge. Nearly overnight, *all* the monkeys on the island began washing their sweet potatoes. Then scientists began reporting that monkeys on other islands had suddenly started washing *their* potatoes! The new knowledge had spread simultaneously, as if by telepathy. This was called the "Hundredth Monkey Phenomenon."

The Hundredth Monkey Phenomenon means that when a few members of a species learn a new way to do something, this knowledge stays only with them. But there is a certain point at which, if only one more member of the species learns this new thing, suddenly all the others know it too. A new field of information is created and it becomes available to others in the species.

A similar observation was reported in Britain when dairies delivered milk in foil-capped bottles. It seems some blue finches learned to peck through the cap to the cream. Other blue finches learned by copying and the trick began to spread slowly. But suddenly, almost overnight, *all* the blue finches throughout the region were pecking through the foil bottle caps.

Rupert Sheldrake, a highly respected British biologist, has suggested that all information fields are interconnected. He believes that it is easier to learn material that has already been learned by others because a resonant "field" gets established by a buildup of experience.

Sheldrake has shown that rats are able to learn a skill more quickly simply because other rats have already learned it. Thus, when one member of a species learns something, it seems that the information becomes available to others through ESP.

Perhaps psychic Alex Tanous is correct in believing that one day science will be able to explain ESP as easily as it now explains how a TV can pick up a picture!

ESP Goes to the Lab

Even though many people have reported ESP experiences, their accounts alone cannot be accepted as proof that ESP does, in fact, exist. Many of the experiments that people have devised in the past to test ESP are not acceptable today.

In 1915, Albert Einstein and Sigmund Freud tested a famous psychic named Wolf Messing. According to Messing, who was only sixteen at the time, the experiment took place in Einstein's apartment. Freud was to give Messing an unspoken, mental command. Einstein would be the witness. After Freud had spent some time concentrating, Messing went into the bathroom and returned, carrying a pair of tweezers. He walked over to Einstein and apologized for what he was about to do, saying he was only carrying out Freud's unspoken orders. He then plucked three hairs from Einstein's moustache! Freud reportedly laughed and told Messing he had carried out his mental command faultlessly.

The problem with this kind of test is that although it makes a charming story, it is impossible to verify. Scientists will not accept reports that cannot be observed, measured and duplicated. For this reason, parapsychologists have been testing ESP using laboratory controls since 1934.

PARAPSYCHOLOGY:
The study of psychic abilities

The Society for Psychical Research was the first parapsychological association. It was formed in London, England, in 1882, and still exists to this day. Duke University in North Carolina was the first university to have a full-time research program on psychic phenomena. This research was begun by Dr. J. B. Rhine in 1934. There are now hundreds of schools and research centres throughout the world that study parapsychology. Dozens of colleges and universities conduct research in the field. The University of Edinburgh in Scotland even offers a Ph.D. program in Parapsychology.

In 1956, The Parapsychological Association was formed. This is an international organization of professional researchers who investigate psi research. The association is affiliated with The American Association for the Advancement of Science, a very highly regarded organization.

The same rigorous standards of research methods that govern the physical sciences are also used in parapsychology. Parapsychologists collect case histories, investigate reports of psychic phenomena and conduct laboratory experiments.

Parapsychologists are not psychic practitioners. They are scientists and academics who do research into psychic phenomena.

Unfortunately, parapsychologists have found it extremely difficult to test ESP under laboratory conditions and get consistent,
reliable results.

WHY IS IT SO DIFFICULT TO TEST FOR ESP?

Because of its very nature, it is difficult to study any psi phenomena under laboratory conditions. ESP is creative and spontaneous; it is not routine and predictable. Researchers have
compared studying psi to the study of zoology, where animals in
the wild behave differently than when they are in an artificial setting, such as a laboratory or a zoo.

ESP is an unconscious process. In this regard, it is similar to
dreaming. Although you can train yourself to have some conscious control over your dreams, you can never control all your
dreams all of the time. Edgar Cayce, the famous psychic whose
ESP abilities have been studied and documented, said, "Sometimes
The Information won't come. It isn't anything I can control."

Scientists once thought that a person with ESP should be able
to perform the same way all the time. But Louisa Rhine, who studied ESP for over forty years with her husband, came to the con-
clusion that ESP can only be present when both conscious and
unconscious conditions are favourable.

Think of it this way: Olympic gold medallist Donovan Bailey
can run 100 metres in 9.84 seconds. But he can't do it every single time he runs. However, the fact that Bailey can't do it every
time − or even most of the time − does not disprove his ability

to run 100 metres in 9.84 seconds.

A United States CIA report, released under the Freedom of Information Act, confirms that government scientists studying highly gifted ESP subjects have had similar difficulties in getting consistent results. The report states, "Due to the elusive, unconscious nature of ESP, these same subjects could not reliably repeat the results and it has not been possible to solve the problem of overcoming this difficulty."

THE FIRST ESP EXPERIMENT

The first recorded ESP experiment took place in Greece in 550 B.C. In those times, priests and priestesses often served as oracles. People believed that oracles were able to communicate with the gods and could answer questions and make predictions. The king of Lydia, however, suspected that some of these oracles were fakes. He decided to conduct an experiment.

The king arranged that on a certain day, messengers would ask the top seven oracles this question: "What is the king of Lydia doing today?" None of the messengers knew what the answer was, so they couldn't cheat. (And remember, this is 550 B.C. — there were no telephones or e-mail then!)

On the appointed day, when he was hundreds of kilometres away, the king decided to do something very unusual. He made a lamb and tortoise stew and cooked it in a bronze kettle.

Six of the seven oracles failed the test. But the Delphic oracle gave the following answer:

Can I not number all the grains of sand,
And measure all the water in the sea?
Tho' a man speak not I can understand;
Nor are the thoughts of dumb men hid from me.
A tortoise boiling with a lamb I smell:
Bronze underlies and covers them as well.

In her time, the oracle of Delphi was so highly regarded that even the great teacher and philospher Socrates consulted her.

HOW SCIENTISTS TEST ESP TODAY

Parapsychologists have devised several standardized experiments to test for ESP.

ZENER CARDS

When J. B. Rhine first began to test ESP in 1934, he used special cards for his experiments. These cards were designed by a Swiss psychologist named Zener. The plain white cards each had a different symbol: a star, a circle, a cross, a square or wavy lines.

There are twenty-five cards to a set: five of each symbol. During an experiment, the subject attempts to predict which card will turn up. At first, some people had amazingly high scores. But after awhile, their scores would decline. This happened over and over

again; the same thing was reported in other laboratories all over the world. This drop in scores is so reliable that parapsychologists call it "the decline effect."

It seems that guessing at cards soon becomes boring. Most ESP subjects agree with test subject Gilbert Murray, who has spent long hours being tested. "I never had any success in guessing mere cards or numbers, or in any subject that was not in some way interesting or amusing."

One time, however, Dr. Rhine was testing a man named Hubert Pearce with the Zener cards. Rhine bet Pearce $100 that he could not guess all the cards. Pearce guessed all twenty-five correctly!

THE GANZFELD TECHNIQUE

In order to see if people had more ESP when they were not distracted by outside stimuli, parapsychologists developed the Ganzfeld technique. Ganzfeld is a German word meaning uniform field.

In this kind of experiment, volunteers recline in comfortable positions in a soundproof, electromagnetically shielded room. Their eyes are covered and bathed with a soft, warm, orange light. Headphones play a gentle hissing sound, called white noise.

In another room, the experimenter selects a slide. It is shown to a person called a sender in a third room. The sender tries to transmit the image telepathically to the subjects. During the session, the subjects describe whatever mental impressions they have. These impressions are recorded and compared with the images sent.

REMOTE VIEWING

In this procedure, researchers are divided into pairs of "viewers" and "beacons." The beacon goes to a particular site, such as a park or harbour. The viewer tries to pick up information about the partner's experience. The viewer gives a verbal description and a sketch to an interviewer, then an impartial judge determines if the descriptions match the sites.

Research shows that this technique has a high success: up to sixty-six percent. This technique has now been replicated in forty-six separate studies. Distances involved varied from one kilometre to several thousand, including one viewer who worked underwater in a submarine!

Those doing the tests say that the best results come from viewers who are relaxed, attentive and meditative. Successful viewing seems to involve a perception of general form rather than precise detail. For example, viewers may draw accurate outlines of a building's shape but may get the number of columns or windows wrong.

The problem with both the Ganzfeld and remote-viewing techniques is that receivers will often wrongly interpret the information they receive. In one experiment, Richard Bach, the author of *Jonathan Livingston Seagull,* interpreted the cross over a church altar as an airline logo!

ANIMAL ESP TESTS

Dogs, cats, rats, goldfish, mice, gerbils and tiny one-celled organisms called paramecia are some of the animals that have been tested for ESP. Some tests seemed to show evidence of animal ESP — until in 1974 an American researcher was caught cheating. Since this researcher had participated in many tests in Europe and the United States, most of the positive data had to be thrown out. Even worse, most researchers were so discouraged by the fraud they stopped testing animals completely. It will take years to retest and accumulate new data.

Some of the animal tests that had been done seem quite humorous. In one experiment, humans concentrated on Zener cards and tried to project the symbols to a dog sitting across the room. The dog sat at a table behind a display of the symbols. Each time the human turned up a new card, the dog was supposed to touch the proper symbol with its paw or nose. As you might expect, most dogs would not co-operate with this kind of test and the experiment was a resounding failure!

THE COCKROACH MAN

Even cockroaches and caterpillars have been tested for ESP! One parapsychologist tried to devise tests to discover if insects could be affected by human telepathy. Unfortunately, for his trouble, the poor man was nicknamed "the cockroach man."

Dr. Helmut Schmidt, a physicist at the Mind Science Foundation in San Antonio, Texas, also experimented with bugs. In one test, he wanted to find out if cockroaches had PK powers. He ran an electric current through a metal grille that was programmed to turn on and off at certain times. Then he put his subjects on it. Schmidt wanted to see if the cockroaches could use PK to shut off the switch that controlled the electric current. To everyone's surprise, the current actually *increased* when the cockroaches were put on the grille! The electric current turned on more times than it was programmed to run. No mechanical reason could be found. Schmidt came up with two possible explanations: perhaps the cockroaches *liked* getting electric shocks and, if so, they were using PK to increase their pleasure. Or perhaps Schmidt himself was using PK to zap the creepy cockroaches!

EMOTION:
The missing ingredient

Since so many ESP experiences are reported at a time of crisis, some researchers believe that ESP is dependent on a strong emotional charge. They think that ESP is an extreme survival ability that is meant to function in a crisis, when normal channels of communication are blocked. Therefore, they argue, it is impossible to reliably test ESP in a laboratory. Guessing at cards in a laboratory is a far cry from sensing that your own child is in danger.

Russian scientists have tried to devise experiments that involve strong emotion. They have carried out several successful telepathic transmissions by focusing on emotions rather than images or thoughts. In one experiment, a sender concentrated on strong, violent emotions. He imagined himself punching and wrestling with his receiver, who successfully got the message! Experiencing emotion through ESP can be especially difficult on test subjects, however. Karl Nikolaiev, a Russian psi research subject, said, "There's one kind of test I really hate. The tests with negative emotions. They sometimes make me sick for hours."

Dr. Bernard Grad says a subject's emotions are critical to the outcome of any experiment. He tells of a healer who was involved in a healing experiment on a rat. Instead of being healed, the rat died. When asked why, the healer replied, "I hate rats!"

Other tests show that if ESP subjects are feeling good, interested and enjoying the tests, they will almost always score higher than if they are unhappy and bored.

It has also been observed that the emotions of other people in research labs can affect the outcome of psi experiments. If researchers are hostile or unfriendly, the test results are always lower than when the experimenters are friendly and positive.

SHEEP AND GOATS

Dr. Gertrude Schmeidler, a psychology professor at Radcliffe and New York City College, asked test subjects whether they believed in ESP or not. She labelled those who did believe as "sheep," and those who didn't, "goats." In a study of over 13 000 ESP tests, she found that sheep always scored higher than random chance would predict, and that goats always scored lower. This strongly suggests that people's beliefs can affect their ESP results.

SET UP YOUR OWN ESP LAB

Throughout this book, you will find descriptions of psi experiments that you can do at home. In addition, you and a friend can easily try any of the techniques described above. But before you start, you should decide whether you and your friends are "sheep" or "goats." This information may be useful to know later on. Here is an easy test you can try right now for fun:

Flip a coin in the air. Before it lands, call it by saying whether it will land heads or tails. Keep track of your hits and misses. The coin has only two sides, therefore the chances are fifty-fifty that it will land on the side that you called. So if you throw the coin fifty times and guess right more than half the time, you could have ESP potential!

CHAPTER 5

Psychic Healing

Psychic healing was likely the first medicine ever practised by men and women in ancient times. Hippocrates, who lived 400 years B.C. and who is considered to be the father of modern medicine, was aware of the healing power of psychic energy: "It has often appeared, while I have been soothing my patient, as if there were some strange property in my hands to pull and draw away from the affected parts aches and diverse impurities."

Jack, who is eighteen, broke his ankle playing ball. When the cast came off, Jack remained in pain, even though his doctor said the ankle had healed perfectly. The pain was so bad that Jack couldn't play any of the sports he loved. Finally, his girlfriend persuaded him to see a psychic healer. Jack says:

> To tell you the truth, I didn't think it would help.
> I just went to please my girlfriend. But it was
> pretty amazing. The healer didn't touch me at all.

She just passed her hands over my body. I could
feel heat coming from her hands, and a few times
I felt a burning around my ankle. But when it
was over, I had no pain in my ankle, and I'm
back playing ball!

Most psychic healing has developed from the ancient practice called the laying on of hands. There are written descriptions of this art that are 5000 years old, and illustrations in cave paintings that date back 15 000 years!

Today, the laying on of hands is often referred to as healing touch. It is a kind of energy transfer that takes place when the healer puts his or her hands on the patient's body. Many healers say they can feel a kind of energy leave their bodies when they work. The patients often feel a tingling or hot sensation where they are touched.

In North America, more than 30 000 health practitioners in hospitals use healing touch or a similar practice called therapeutic touch. Therapeutic touch began when Dolores Krieger, a nursing researcher, discovered that when sick people were treated by the laying on of hands, their hemoglobin levels increased. This is important because hemoglobin increases the oxygen-carrying capacity of the blood. More hemoglobin means that every cell in the body receives more nourishment.

Other studies show that therapeutic touch reduces pain and speeds healing in patients. In some patients, brain tumours shrink and even disappear.

The amazing thing about therapeutic touch is that the practitioner seldom touches the patient's physical body. Instead, the caregiver holds his or her hands a few centimetres away from the patient. Eighteen-year-old Beverly says:

> *The nurse didn't touch me, but I could feel a kind of warmth, or heat, moving through my body. Sometimes different parts of my body got hot, almost like they were burning. Afterwards I felt really calm and relaxed.*

Through training, the practitioner is able to sense where problems are located in the patient's body. Although some practitioners may actually touch the spot, most hold their hands over the affected area and focus on it. You will learn how to sense your own energy field in Chapter 13, Develop Your ESP Potential.

Dr. Bernard Grad, whom you read about earlier, conducted a well-documented experiment using healing touch: A group of mice had small wounds made in their skin. Some mice received no treatment at all. Some were held twice a day by psychic healer Oskar Estebany. Mice in the third group were held by students for an equal length of time. The mice held by Estebany recovered much faster than the others.

In another experiment, barley seeds given water treated by therapeutic touch sprouted at a faster rate, grew higher, and produced plants that contained more chlorophyll than the seeds of a control group.

In the United States, Dr. Daniel Worth conducted an amazing experiment. Volunteers were told they would be part of a study to test a new, super-sensitive camera. Doug was one of the participants. He said:

We all had a small incision made on our forearms. Then we were divided into two groups. Each person had to put their cut arm into a hole in the wall and sit for five minutes. We did that every day for a week.

The hole was heavily draped so that nothing was visible on the other side. Each volunteer sat for exactly five minutes and was told that a special camera was filming the wound to see if it could record any aura around it.

In reality, there was no such camera. Half of the volunteers simply sat with their arms hanging in empty space. The other half of the group unknowingly had their arms exposed to a psychic healing session conducted by a healer named Laurie Eden.

When the experiment ended, the group that was exposed to the healer had either healed completely, or were healing faster than those in the control group.

Lucy Maud Montgomery, the author of *Anne of Green Gables*, knew about the relationship between mind and matter. In her personal journal she described how she prepared herself for the birth of her baby:

A few years ago I read Hudson's Law of Psychic
Phenomena. *Ever since, I have had a strong
belief in the power which the subconscious mind
can exert over physical functions. Every night, as
I was dropping off to sleep, and frequently
through the day, I repeated over and over the
command to my subconscious mind, "Make my
child strong and healthy in mind and body and
make his birth safe and painless for me." . . .
His birth was safe and painless for me . . . I
believe it was the psychic suggestion which
produced my easy time.*

These examples are important because they show us that
thought can produce changes in matter, our bodies.

HEALING AND PRAYER

Another scientific experiment showed that people who were
prayed for recovered better and faster than people who were not
prayed for.

This study was done with 393 heart patients at a hospital in San
Francisco. Half the patients were prayed for; the other half, called
the control group, were not. None of the patients knew which
group they were in. The prayed-for group suffered fewer compli-
cations in three areas. Only three required antibiotics, compared
to sixteen in the control group. Only six suffered pulmonary
edema (waterlogging of the lungs), compared to eighteen of the

There have been other reports of psychic surgeons who have removed tumours and other growths from patients without using medical instruments or anaesthesia, but investigation has shown that these surgeries were tricks. The surgeons used animal blood and sleight of hand to stage fake operations.

ESP and Dreams

If only the great singer and musician Buddy Holly had listened to his dreams, he might still be alive and making music today. Days before his last concert trip began, both Buddy and his wife Maria Elena dreamed about terrible disasters on the very same night. The next morning, Maria Elena begged Buddy not to go ahead with the planned tour. But because he needed the money, Buddy decided to proceed, despite his misgivings. A few days later, Buddy Holly was killed in a plane crash, along with musicians Richie Valens and The Big Bopper.

Studies have shown that about two-thirds of all spontaneous incidents of ESP happen in dreams. As you read earlier, a relaxed and open mind is the most likely receptor of ESP waves. Sigmund Freud agreed, saying, "It is an uncontestable fact that sleep creates favourable conditions for telepathy."

Dreams that involve some kind of ESP date back as early as recorded history. There are several examples in the Bible. The king of Egypt's dream of seven thin cows eating seven fat cows is probably the best known. It correctly predicted there would be seven years of abundance, followed by seven years of famine.

Many people have reported dreaming about a disaster before it happened. Unfortunately, it is usually not possible to verify these accounts because they are reported after the fact. As shown in Chapter 2, premonition registries try to address this problem by recording premonitions before they happen. The Central Premonitions Registry in New York City exists because of a precognitive dream.

In May, 1968, Alan Vaughan dreamed that an assassination attempt would be made on Robert Kennedy in a hallway leading into a kitchen. Vaughan described his dream in a letter to dream researcher Stanley Krippner, and asked Krippner to warn Kennedy, if he could, because, "If it happened, I think I should have it on my conscience; if it doesn't, then I only need feel a bit foolish."

A few days later, Robert Kennedy was assassinated in the hallway of a hotel kitchen. Within the month, Robert Nelson, a former executive at the *New York Times,* began publicizing the Central Premonitions Registry. He hoped that if he received several independent warnings of the same disaster, he might be able to alert those at risk.

One of the first people to actually collect precognitive dream information was the brilliant aeronautics engineer J. W. Dunne, who designed and built the first British military aircraft. In his book *Experiment With Time,* Dunne described how he dreamed one night that his watch stopped at half-past four and that a crowd of people was shouting, "Look! Look!" He awoke to discover it *was* half-past four and that his watch *had* stopped. This was the first of many precognitive dreams he had that convinced him the human mind could foresee the future.

Another man's dream helped him save his own life. The man dreamed that a bridge collapsed as a train was crossing over it, plunging all the passengers to their deaths. The next day, the man had to travel by train across the same bridge. At the last stop before the bridge, he got off. As soon as the train moved onto the bridge, it collapsed, just as his dream had predicted.

Dr. Ian Stevenson, a Canadian researcher, has documented nineteen different cases of ESP connected to the sinking of the *Titanic*. One of these cases concerned a woman who lived in New York. One night the woman had a terrible dream that her mother was packed into a crowded lifeboat in the middle of a freezing sea. When she awoke, she was convinced something terrible had happened to her mother. Her husband tried to reassure her that her mother was safe in England. But the woman was certain this was more than a dream.

The next day, the woman discovered that her mother was in fact on a freezing lifeboat at the very moment she'd had her dream. The mother wanted to surprise her daughter, and had booked passage on the *Titanic* without telling her!

Before his assassination, the great American president Abraham Lincoln had this dream:

> *I was walking from room to room in the White*
> *House. I saw no one, but everywhere I heard*
> *sobbing. Finally I arrived at the east room*
> *where there was a coffin on a platform. It was*
> *surrounded by soldiers. Behind it was a crowd*
> *of weeping people. "Who is dead in the White*
> *House?" I asked one of the guards. "The*
> *President," came the answer. "He was*
> *assassinated."*

A few days later Abraham Lincoln was shot and killed by John Wilkes Booth.

Although death and distress seem to be the most common themes reported in dream ESP, good news comes as well. Pearl Anderson, a grandmother and nurse's aide who lives in California, had the following experience:

> *I dreamed of buckets of money pouring out of a*
> *slot machine. I told my husband about it and he*
> *said, "Well, you'd better go to Reno." I left for*
> *Reno after work, and got there around two*
> *o'clock in the morning. I went straight to the*
> *slot machines. On my second try at the three-*
> *dollar "Millionaire" slot machine, five sevens*
> *came up on the register, bells and buzzers*
> *sounded and people started clapping and*
> *cheering.*

Anderson won a million dollars! It was the first million-dollar payoff for the machine since it had been installed three years earlier, and the largest at the casino in five years.

John Godley, a university student, also got good news. On a Friday night he dreamed:

> *I read the racing results in Saturday's evening*
> *paper. Two horses, named Bindal and Tuladin,*
> *had both won at seven to one. The next day,*
> *Saturday, I went to the race-track and found that*
> *there were indeed two horses called Bindal and*
> *Tuladin running that day. I placed bets on the*
> *horses, and to my amazement and delight, they*
> *each placed first!*

Godley had many other dreams that also came true. On one occasion he wrote down a prediction about a horse race, had it timed, witnessed and taken to a post office, where it was sealed in an envelope, stamped by the postmaster and locked up in a post office safe. Both his horses won as predicted.

Mrs. Forgie, a Toronto woman, also received racing tips through her dreams. A few days before a race she would dream of the winner. Often, these horses were longshots that paid out very high winnings.

More recently, a woman's brand new car was stolen. She was terribly upset, and that night, an amazing series of events began: The woman's daughter dreamed that she saw the car in a very specific location. The dream was so vivid that the next morning, the daughter persuaded her husband to drive to the place she'd dreamed about. When they arrived, they found the car exactly as she had dreamed. Witnesses said the car had been left in that spot only minutes before the woman and her husband arrived.

Sometimes it is difficult to know if a dream is predicting or inspiring the dreamer to make it come true. The award-winning Canadian fashion designer Wayne Clark dreamed about a beautiful jacket with intricate panels sewn into it. He says:

> *I thought about the jacket in my dream all*
> *weekend, thinking how would I do that? I went*
> *to work on Monday and I tried and it worked and*
> *it wasn't even as hard as I thought it would be.*

Would you call Clark's dream precognition or inspiration? Perhaps it is both.

Here's quite a different ESP dream, this time about something that happened in the past.

Some years ago in North Carolina a man named James Chaffin died. He left a will giving all of the family property to only one of his four sons. The three disinherited sons could do nothing because the will was witnessed and legal. But then one of the disinherited sons had the following dream:

> *My father appeared and in the dream he told*
> *me there was another will. He told me to look*

in the pocket of an old overcoat that was
in my brother's house.

The brothers found the overcoat. One of the pockets had been stitched closed. They opened up the pocket and found a paper. On the paper was a reference to a page in the family Bible. In the Bible, there was a second will, in the father's handwriting, stating that he wished his property to be shared by his four sons.

Now, it's certainly possible that one of the sons made the whole thing up. Maybe he planted the note in the coat pocket, stitched it up and put a forged will in the family Bible. However, the North Carolina State Court believed the dream and the evidence, and accepted the second will as valid.

Another case of dream precognition was reported by the American writer Mark Twain. He dreamed he saw his dead brother Henry laid out in the sitting room, in a metallic coffin set on two chairs, a bouquet of flowers on his chest, with a single red blossom in the centre. On awakening, Twain told his sister about the dream. Weeks later, Twain's brother Henry was killed in an explosion. When Twain viewed his brother's body, it was exactly as he had dreamed it, except there was no bouquet on Henry's chest. But as he was standing next to the body, a woman entered the room and laid on Henry's chest a bouquet of white flowers with a red rose in the centre.

In August, 1883, a Boston newspaper reporter named Edward Samson fell asleep at his desk. At three o'clock in the morning he awoke after this terrible dream:

Alexander concentrated on maps of the area. She pointed out one particular place and said,

> *The body is here. The head and left foot are*
> *separated from the body. One of the arms is*
> *broken. There is a three-inch split in the skull.*
> *A rib is broken and there is a fracture in the*
> *right leg. The man who will find the body has a*
> *bad hand — it has been injured.*

A second search of the area was conducted. Soon after the officers began digging, the bones of a human foot were uncovered. Further digging revealed a complete skeleton. The body was exactly as Alexander had described. The officer who first uncovered the body was named Scott Trew. Years before, he had been injured in an accident. The accident had deformed Trew's left hand!

A squad commander with the New York Police Department states: "Police officers are naturally skeptical of psychics and psychic phenomena . . . However, the use of a psychic can be considered as an additional investigative aid."

When Samuel Bronfman, the Seagram's heir, was kidnapped in New York City, police asked Uri Geller for help. Geller was a well-known Israeli psychic who was being tested by American scientists. At the time, Geller was visiting New York and was able to correctly identify the area in Brooklyn where Bronfman was eventually found.

Even though psi is often helpful, some police officers are reluctant to turn to psychics for help because it can often be a waste of time and money. One detective who will no longer work with psychics complained, "We spent hundreds of man-hours running around where these people were telling us to go. At the same time, we weren't doing the things we should have been doing to bring the case to court." But some police officials still find it helpful to consult with psychics when an investigation has come to a dead end.

On a farm north of Edmonton, Alberta, a man named Vernon Booher discovered the dead bodies of his mother, brother and two farmhands. After six months of investigation that led nowhere, the Edmonton chief of police contacted Dr. Maximillian Langsner. The doctor had become well known after using his ESP to solve a robbery in Vancouver, British Columbia. Langsner consulted with the chief and, using his ESP, identified Vernon Booher as the murderer. He also described where the missing murder weapon was hidden, at the back of the house.

The next day, Langsner accompanied the police officers to the farm. He told them to look in a particular spot. Almost immediately, a rifle was found. When tested, it was found to be the rifle used in the shootings.

Langsner had also learned through his ESP that Booher was worried about an old woman who had seen him sneak out of church when he had gone to steal the rifle used in the killings.

A meeting was arranged between the woman and Booher. The woman told Booher she had seen him leave church the same day

Crowds of people were rushing towards the sea.
They were running from an ocean of boiling lava.
Ships were crushed beneath huge waves, and
then a volcano erupted and destroyed the entire
island. There were terrible screams as the people
were buried in the lava.

The dream was so vivid that Samson wrote it down and left the paper by his desk. The next day his editor published the story, thinking that it was a real event. You can imagine Samson's embarrassment when he had to explain that the story was only a dream. But a few days later it was learned that the volcanic island of Krakatoa, in Java, had exploded the same night that Samson had had his dream! More than 36 000 people were killed, and dozens of ships had been sunk by a tidal wave.

Precognitive dreams can happen anywhere – even in prison! In 1885, John Lee was sentenced to be hanged at Exeter Prison in England. The night before the scheduled hanging, Lee had the following dream:

I was taken from my cell down through a
basement corridor to the gallows, where I was
placed on the drop [the trap door] and kept
waiting there because the mechanism opening
the drop would not work. Finally, I was taken
by another route back to my cell.

In the morning, Lee told his dream to the assistant warden and to the supervising officer. These two officers reported the dream to the governor. The rest of the morning's events happened as in the dream. Lee could not be hanged and was finally taken back to his cell. Records note that mechanical failures were rare at the time, and Lee had never seen the route he described in his dream.

Lee's death sentence was withdrawn and he was given life imprisonment. After serving fifteen years, Lee went to America, where he lived another forty years.

The dreams I have just described are called spontaneous ESP occurrences. This means that the dreamers had spontaneous experiences of ESP without consciously trying to do so. People can, however, with a little patience and practice, train themselves to deliberately have telepathic dreams! In many of my dream study groups, participants could transmit images or thoughts to each other via their dreams. As well, members often reported dreaming about the same things.

For many years, Dr. Stanley Krippner has conducted research into dream telepathy at the Dream Laboratory of the Maimonides Medical Center in Brooklyn, New York. His experiments show that dreams can be influenced telepathically. Images or concepts can be transmitted from a waking "sender" to a dreaming "receiver."

Dreams can and do bring us much valuable information and knowledge. What about your own dreams? If you keep a dream journal, you may find that some of your own dreams involve ESP!

CHAPTER 8

Psychic Spies

Many countries try to find out secret information about their enemies and allies by spying on them. In addition to the usual methods of spying, however, some intelligence agencies actually employ psychic spies!

In 1991, *The Globe and Mail*'s USSR bureau reported that Boris Yeltsin's security staff used a psychic to supplement their normal methods of protection. When Yeltsin's staff believed that the KGB had electronically bugged their offices, a psychic was brought to the Russian president's suite. The psychic used his ESP to scan the rooms of Yeltsin and his staff and he reassured them that the area was secure.

The CIA has been conducting psi spy research for years. In November 1996, the agency released documents spanning over twenty years of covert support. One secret memorandum, recently released under the U.S. Freedom of Information Act, states:

If a subject under control test conditions can identify the order of a deck of cards several hundred yards away in another building, or can identify the thought of another person several hundred miles away . . . obtaining secret information should not give serious difficulty.

In 1977 the CIA admitted it had financed a program called Star Gate to develop the talents of a psychic agent who could "see" events and places anywhere in the world. Victor Marchetti, a former CIA employee, has written about some of these ESP experiments. According to Marchetti, "There is no indication that they [the CIA] have stopped, and no reason why they would."

Former U.S. President Jimmy Carter has confirmed that the CIA used ESP during his presidency. In 1995 he publicly stated that psychics were used to locate an airplane that had been lost in Zaire. In a Czech military handbook called *Clairvoyance, Hypnotism and Magnetic Healing at the Service of the Military,* the author describes using the telepathic powers of two soldiers to learn about the enemy's strength and position. Bulgaria has two Institutes of Suggestology and Parapsychology. The Bulgarian secret police includes trained clairvoyants and telepaths on its staff.

Russia has more than twenty centres for the study of paranormal phenomena. In the late 1970s Robert Toth, a reporter for the *Los Angeles Times,* was arrested by KGB agents after he had been given a scientific paper by the Russian biophysicist Valery

were living there. When police searched the apartment, they discovered the kidnapped boy, frightened but unharmed.

Although Palmer went on to help police in several other cases, he found that his gift exposed him to too much misery and suffering. Eventually he withdrew from police work and became a recluse. He never helped with another case.

Many professional psychics avoid police work for the same reason. It is usually unpleasant and distressing. Many psychics say it's as if they experience the crime themselves, and feel the pain and suffering of the victims. Some are afraid. Many psychics say they have been threatened or attacked while consulting on police cases. Others, like Czech psychic Frederick Marion, feel police work is an exercise in frustration. He says that "working with the police is a very thankless task. If a psychic succeeded, police were unwilling to admit that any psychic guidance was responsible. But if the psychic failed, the police would abuse him with ridicule and blame."

But ridicule and blame can seem minor when compared to another psychic's experience. Etta Smith was arrested and accused of committing the very crime she had described to police! Smith was a young mother living in Los Angeles, California. After hearing a news story about a young woman who had disappeared, Smith had a vision of the young woman's murdered body. She could "see" the body hidden in a particular part of a canyon and was able to note the exact area from the vegetation and rock formations.

Although she was afraid the police would think she was crazy,

Smith drove to the nearest police station. The vision had been so strong, she was convinced she must speak. A police officer listened to Smith, asked her more questions and filed a report. They decided that she was a crank, and her claims were not investigated.

The next day, Smith's children persuaded her to drive out to the canyon to see if she could find the place she had seen in her vision. She did so, and discovered the murdered woman's body exactly as she had seen it. Frightened and panicked, Smith drove away with her children and found a police officer. The policeman followed her back to the site.

The police then began to suspect Smith because she had described details that only the murderer could know. She was held in custody for four days and told that she was to be charged with murder!

In the meantime, because police believed that Smith was guilty, there was no search for the real killer. By chance, a patrolman stopped a speeding car. When the officer ran a routine check on the car, he discovered that it belonged to the dead woman. The driver was detained. Thinking the police were on to him, the driver panicked and made a full confession, naming two other men as his accomplices. Only then was Smith released.

Etta Smith sued the city of Los Angeles for the trauma she suffered from her treatment by the police. Not surprisingly, although she won her case, she never offered her help to police again.

Difficult and unrewarding as police work may be, many psychics feel they have a responsibility to come forward to offer their help. But whether they have had good or bad experiences working with police, all psychics agree that ESP has no place in court. Cases must be judged only on hard evidence. ESP may be a helpful tool in gaining evidence, but it must never *become* evidence. Frederick Marion, the Czech psychic, contends that, "I do not believe ESP impressions can be used as evidence in criminology. I do believe that they can be used as directions for scientific investigation, as they may well open up avenues not previously considered by the police."

Not many people know that a clairvoyant was consulted when Quebec separatists kidnapped James Cross and Pierre Laporte during the October Crisis in 1970. The Front de Libération du Québec was a group of terrorists whose violence, bombings and kidnapping caused a national crisis in Canada. Members of the FLQ kidnapped James Cross, a British trade representative, and Pierre Laporte, the Quebec Minister of Labour. Laporte was murdered by his kidnappers.

Irene Hughes, an American psychic who was called "the Queen of Psychic Chicago," was interviewed on a live radio program on October 14, 1970. She predicted that Laporte would be physically harmed but that Cross would not suffer the same fate. She said that the kidnappers would be arrested in two or three months and that something very important would happen on November 6.

Hughes was interviewed again on October 18. She felt that Cross was still alive, though very weak and ill. She said that he was being held captive somewhere northwest of Montreal and she described the building he was in. Four more interviews were taped with the psychic during this time, but according to interviewer

Robert Cummings, at the request of "the authorities," these were not broadcast until later. On November 6, Bernard Lortie confessed to his part in the crimes. Hughes had been had been right on all counts.

There is no doubt that ESP has provided some amazingly accurate and helpful information to the police. The next chapter, Psychic Spies, will take you into an even more complex world of ESP, mystery and intrigue.

Petukhov. This secret paper dealt with the potential of "information transfer," or telepathy, between cell particles or photons. Toth was accused of receiving state secrets about parapsychology. After a lengthy interrogation, he was sent back to the United States.

FAMOUS PSI SPIES

In the past, rulers of many countries employed psychic spies in addition to their regular spies. History is full of accounts of military leaders and political rulers who used soothsayers, "seers" and clairvoyants to spy psychically on enemies and to predict and even alter the outcomes of battles and events.

In the Bible, Elisha's "psychic" viewings of Syrian troop movements saved Israel from military defeat. It also made the King of Syria mistrustful of his own troops. He believed that one of his men must be a traitor and a spy.

STALIN'S PERSONAL PSI SPY

After the Communist Revolution in Russia, there was a taboo against all things psychic. According to the official Soviet encyclopedia, ESP was an "anti-social, idealist fiction."

In spite of this, a psychic named Wolf Messing became a huge success in the Soviet Union. He was born in Poland but when Hitler came to power, Messing fled to the USSR by hiding in a wagonload of hay.

Messing became a kind of psi superstar who demonstrated his remarkable powers of ESP and hypnosis in performances all over the world. Many scholars interviewed and tested him. He met

Einstein, Freud and Gandhi, and successfully passed the tests that these great thinkers devised.

Messing described how he experienced ESP this way: "People's thoughts come to me as pictures. I usually see visual images of a specific action or place."

Joseph Stalin, the Soviet dictator, was intrigued by Messing's talents. He was especially attracted by the psychic's ability to change other people's perceptions by telepathy or suggestion. Stalin was impressed when Messing "willed" a teller in the state bank to give him a large sum of money in exchange for a blank piece of paper. Stalin was persuaded that Messing could control the thoughts of others and make them see what he wished them to see. According to Messing himself, he was able to use his telepathic powers to "cloud men's minds." As a result of his power, Messing was held in great favour by Stalin. Stalin used Messing to spy psychically on his enemies and as an oracle to predict the outcome of military events.

Wolf Messing predicted that Hitler would die and his army would be defeated. This so upset Hitler that he put a price on Messing's head — 200 000 marks! In spite of the bounty on him, Messing survived the war unscathed.

NAZIS AND ESP

Hitler also had a psychic spy. Erik Jan Hanussen was a clairvoyant who became highly influential among leading members of Germany's Nazi party. He received international publicity after correctly predicting the terrible Reichstag fire in Germany, and became hugely successful and powerful. He lived in a fourteen-room mansion he called "The Palace of Occultism" in Berlin and owned a lavish white yacht.

Even though Hanussen was Jewish, he sometimes dressed in a Nazi storm trooper uniform, complete with swastika armband. He even had his own personal group of twenty-five Nazi storm trooper bodyguards! He called himself the "Rasputin of the Reich," and was involved with the secret police.

His psychic powers, however, eventually led to his downfall. Because he could "see" the Nazis' secret projects, he became a threat to them. One evening, after he gave a performance at the opera house, the secret police came for him at home and hustled him into a waiting car. Hanussen's body was found two weeks later in the woods outside of Berlin. He had been shot five times.

The Nazis also hunted and executed the Polish psychic Stefan Ossowiecki. Ossowiecki had used his psi powers to aid the Polish underground. Among his feats was the ability to locate specific bodies that were buried in mass graves.

SPY WITH A CONSCIENCE

Captain Nicolai Khokhlov was an agent in the Soviet KGB's Division for Terror and Diversion, also known as the murder squad. Unknown to his superiors, Khokhlov began to develop a conscience – he became sickened by the cruel and immoral things he was ordered to do. Finally, in 1954, when he was ordered to "silence" an innocent man, Khokhlov decided he'd had enough. He went to the intended victim's home and confessed he'd been sent to kill him! Khokhlov then defected to the United States and became a professor of psychology at California State University.

Khokhlov revealed many secrets about the KGB, including valuable information about psychic espionage. He described secret Russian experiments involving psi abilities on a large scale. He also revealed experiments that used telepathy and other psi methods to stop the heartbeats of animals.

HER MAJESTY'S SECRET PSI SERVICE

Everybody has heard of James Bond, the fictional Agent 007 in Her Majesty's Secret Service. But did you know that in the sixteenth century, Queen Elizabeth I had a secret *psychic* agent? His name was John Dee and he was the queen's mathematician and astrologer. By giving psychic readings for European nobles, John Dee was able to gather important information for the queen. He advised Elizabeth on exploration ventures and accurately foretold that the Spanish would build large ships to attack England. Dee used a medium to communicate with spirits who told him about plots and intrigues on the Continent. The medium used a complex system to code information. And John Dee's code name? This is true – it was 007!

Ian Fleming, the creator of the James Bond character, worked for British Naval Intelligence during World War II. During the war, the Nazis established what was called the Pendulum Institute in Berlin to provide psychic information for German Naval Intelligence. Pendulum swingers would hold a pendulum over a map and dowse for enemy ships. (Dowsing, the ability to find hid-

mind is not located only in the brain. Her research has led her to conclude that "mind exists in every living cell."

PSYCHIC SURGERY

In 1950, an uneducated Brazilian man named José Arigo claimed that he had been taken over by the spirit of Dr. Fritz, a German surgeon who died in World War I. According to Arigo, Dr. Fritz appeared one night and told him that he was going to cure the sick through him. Arigo began to go into trances in which he carried out medical operations using ordinary scissors and knives. Witnesses said he looked stunned and spoke with a German accent. Afterwards, he could not remember performing the surgery.

Arigo discovered his talent when he visited a dying woman. During the visit, he suddenly went into a trance, rushed from the room and returned with a large knife. In front of horrified friends and family, he plunged the knife into the woman. He twisted the knife and pulled out a huge growth. The local doctor was summoned and carefully examined the woman. There was no hemorrhaging, but the growth removed was a cancerous uterine tumour. The woman rapidly returned to health.

Dr. Ary Lex, a distinguished surgeon and lecturer at the University of Sao Paolo in Brazil, witnessed one of Arigo's operations. He described the scene:

> *In a cramped, grubby kitchen, Arigo cut cataracts*
> *out of the eyes of an old woman using a pair*

*of unsterilized nail scissors. He used no
disinfectant, no anaesthetic and wiped the
scissors on his sport shirt when he had finished.
The operation was over in a few seconds. There
was no blood and no sign of discomfort from
the fully conscious patient. I can testify that
the surgery was a success, and that the woman
regained her sight.*

Although he could have become very rich, Arigo never accepted payment from anyone for his medical services. He performed thousands of complex operations with table knives or scissors in completely unsterile conditions. He cured people thought to be beyond help, until his death in a car crash in 1971.

In Canada, many native medicine men were also accomplished healers. Their powers were recorded by some of the Jesuit priests who observed them. One priest wrote:

*I have seen medicine tested in the most
conclusive ways. I once saw a Kootenai Indian
command a mountain sheep to fall dead, and
the animal, then leaping among the rocks of the
mountainside, fell instantly lifeless. This I saw
with my own eyes, and I ate of the animal
afterwards. It was unwounded, healthy and
perfectly wild.*

control group. None of the prayed-for patients required the insertion of breathing tubes, compared to twelve of the others.

Distance made no difference. While all the patients were in San Francisco, the people who prayed were in different parts of the country. Some were thousands of kilometres away on the east coast.

THE DOCTOR-HEALER NETWORK

Many doctors recognize that psychic or spiritual healers can help traditional medicine work better and faster for their patients. In Britain, more than 1500 psychic healers work co-operatively with medical staff in hospitals.

The Doctor-Healer Network is made up of physicians who practise conventional medicine but have one or more healers working in partnership with them. Lorraine Ham, a healer who works in a clinic with eight doctors and four nurses, says, "It's complementary to what the doctors do, not an alternative. If I had a diseased appendix, I would still want a competent doctor to take it out."

All the doctors in this network agree that more of their patients are getting well and staying well since healers have joined their practices.

THE PLACEBO EFFECT:
Psi at work

In medical experiments, one group of volunteers is given an actual drug and another group is given a sugar pill, or placebo. People who get the placebos often report feeling better. Researchers once maintained that the patient's belief that he or she was receiving real medicine would make them feel feel better, but that no actual physical changes would occur in their bodies. Studies now show, however, that when subjects are given placebos, their belief that they are getting real medicine can sometimes stimulate real, physical changes in their bodies.

Dr. Nicholas Voudouris of La Trobe University in Australia has found that people could mentally recall the relief they received with painkillers, and could recreate the medicine's effect using their own mind power. He says that given the right conditioning, he can make nearly everyone respond to a placebo.

According to Robert Ader, a psychologist at the University of Rochester in New York, just thinking about relief can make the body create natural healing substances. In other words, your own psi can stimulate your body to make its own medicine. Psi can also boost the performance of your immune system, as the following example shows.

In Russian experiments, the number of white blood cells in subjects rose significantly after positive emotions were suggested to the subjects. When negative emotions were suggested, the number of white cells (which help fight infection in the body) decreased.

Although researchers still do not understand how psi can affect the body, research has proven conclusively that it does. Dr. Candace Pert, a biochemist and molecular biologist, is one of the world's leading authorities on brain chemistry. She says that the

CHAPTER 7

ESP Detectives

ESP can actually help solve crimes. In fact, there are many well-documented cases that have been resolved due to psi. Although it is not well known, psychics have lectured at the FBI Academy, as well as to other national law enforcement agencies in the United States. The California Department of Justice recommends using psychics and ESP as a supplement to normal police investigation methods for unusual or difficult cases.

That is exactly what police in Freeport, Maine, did when an eight-year-old boy was reported missing. The police had no clues at all. In desperation, the chief of police called in psychic Alex Tanous to consult on the case.

The police took Tanous to the apartment where John, the missing boy, had lived. The psychic spoke to John's parents and then spent some time in the boy's room. He tried to absorb something of John from the room. Then Tanous asked police to drive him around the area. But as they began to drive away from the building, the psychic shook his head. After several attempts, Tanous explained that as they drove away from the building, the trail went cold. But he was unable to tell where in the building the child could be. Then Tanous explained that he thought the reason he could not pick up anything more about John was because the boy was dead. He felt that the body was wrapped up and hidden beneath something, but he could go no further.

The next day, Tanous was overwhelmed by an image of a face that he had never seen before. He sketched the face and showed it to the police chief. The chief was able to match Tanous's sketch with a photograph from police files. In fact, the sketch was almost a perfect replica of the photograph.

The man in the photgraph lived in the same apartment building as John. He had been a suspect, but was discounted because he had an alibi. When the police obtained a search warrant, they discovered the boy's body wrapped in a blanket and hidden under the bed.

According to psychologist and psychic researcher Dr. Louise Ludwig, "In every police department there is at least one cop who is in touch with a psychic."

Police in Alton, Illinois, consulted Greta Alexander in an unsolved missing persons case. Alexander had developed her ESP powers after being struck by lightning.

When police requested her help, Alexander told them she didn't know if she could help or not. She could not control what came to her; she might not be able to help at all. However, she agreed to try.

the rifle was stolen. Booher replied, "I know you did." Then he whispered, "I killed them all." With the help of Langsner's remarkable ESP powers, Vernon Booher was tried and convicted of murder. He was hanged for his crimes.

In another dramatic case, a psychic named John Catchings was credited by Texas police with finding the body of a seventy-four-year-old woman who had been missing for six weeks. Catchings held a ring that belonged to the missing woman and walked over the fields where her car had been found. He pointed to an area and told police to search there. The deputy sheriff later reported, "I just threw up my hands in disgust because I had been searching there for six weeks."

The area was searched again and the woman's body was discovered less than 100 metres from where Catchings had indicated.

Psychics can specialize in certain kinds of cases. Some are better at locating missing children or lost pets. Others, like Judy Belle, can recreate and describe crime scenes. Police in California have credited Belle's contributions, saying her accuracy is tremendous. Belle herself says,

I can't find anything. I only deal with feelings.
Just once I would love to get a name or an
address but I never do.

Nancy Czetli also has the ability to reconstruct crime scenes. In one murder case, police had thirty-two suspects but no clues. Czetli was able to tell police that the victim knew the killer well and had even been his babysitter. She felt that the killer was a drug addict and that the murder had happened during an argument about money. From a stack of police photographs, Czeti picked the one she felt had a thought pattern most similar to the killer's. Further investigation led to this man's arrest and conviction. According to one of the detectives on the case:

It would have taken us six months to get statements from those thirty-two suspects and then verify their alibis. [The killer] was way down at the bottom of our list. We wouldn't have got to him for months, and by that time who knows where he might have gone?

In South Africa, Nelson Palmer used his ESP to help police find several missing persons. The retired headmaster had developed an ability in psychometry. When he held objects belonging to a missing person, Palmer would see visions that often provided valuable clues to police.

In one case, a family asked Palmer to help them locate their six-year-old son who had been kidnapped. Palmer held a piece of the boy's clothing and began to describe an apartment building with a particular neon sign. A police officer recognized the sign and was able to locate the building. Palmer also described the two kidnappers, a man and a woman. Through his descriptions, the police recognized the man, who was well known to them. They went to the apartment building and learned that the suspect and his wife

den objects using ESP, is explained further in Chapter 12, Apply Your Psi.) Fleming planted a false story that British Intelligence was using its own pendulum swingers to track German U-boats. This story circulated at a time when many German submarines had been sunk, reinforcing the Nazis' belief that the British had a secret psychic weapon!

Other psychic agents were at work during World War II. According to secret documents recently released by the British Army, Lady Dowling, the wife of a top Royal Air Force officer, used remote viewing to accurately locate secret enemy air bases.

In 1944 Helen Duncan, a mother of six, claimed she had contacted the spirit of a sailor killed on *HMS Barham*. Since the sinking of the *Barham* was a military secret, authorities were afraid that Duncan might have psychic knowledge of other government secrets. She was actually convicted of witchcraft and served nine months in prison! For the past fifty years, supporters have been trying to clear Duncan's name. Duncan's case led to the eventual repeal of Britain's Witchcraft Act in 1951.

PSYCHIC WARFARE

In addition to government intelligence agencies, military groups also try to develop and use psi as a military weapon.

A 1966 Czech military journal reveals that the Czech army has frequently used psi for war. Although current information is classified, it has been confirmed that in 1919, soldiers with ESP ability who were put into trance were able to describe the exact position of enemy troops. They also located lost soldiers.

In addition, the army used dowsers to locate traps, weapons and drinking water. Dowsers were able to track the enemy precisely. The army journal *Periskop* stated, "The Czech army achieved extraordinary results with psi which have been concretely confirmed in fighting practice."

Both the United States and Russia look for ways to use ESP in their weapons of war. A U.S. Defense Department report says the Russian military and the KGB are working hard "to harness the possible capabilities of telepathic communications, telekinetics and bionics."

One controversial Russian experiment reportedly used telepathic brain signals to pass messages to a fleet of submarines. In this experiment, baby rabbits were taken down into a submarine while the mother rabbit was kept on land. Radio waves cannot pass through deep water, but the Russians found that the brain waves of rabbits could. They killed the baby rabbits one by one and measured the mother's brain activity. At each death there was a definite reaction from the mother rabbit that, theoretically, could have been used to trigger an electrical switch. If brain waves could travel through water and trigger an electrical switch, scientists believed that it might be possible to develop a form of "mental radio."

In 1977 the United States conducted its own ESP experiment aboard a submarine. The *Taurus* was sent out to sea and then submerged. In San Francisco, 800 kilometres away, two other experimenters visited target sites at pre-arranged times. These two "beacons" concentrated on sending back to the "receiver" what they saw. In the submarine, the receiver, a psychic, was able to correctly describe the target sites.

The *Military Review,* the journal of the U.S. Army, has published articles on the wartime use of ESP. One article, "The New Mental Battlefield" states,

> It has been demonstrated that certain persons
> appear to have the ability to retrieve data from
> afar while physically remaining in a secure
> position . . . Other mind-to-mind thought
> induction techniques are also being considered.
> If perfected, this ability could allow the direct
> transference of thought, via telepathy, from one
> mind or group of minds to a selected target
> audience.

David Morehouse, a former military officer, has described his experiences as a "remote viewer" for the U.S. Army. The training program, named Sun Streak, attempted to collect secret data using ESP. Morehouse and other viewers were trained to use their minds to transcend time and space. Their goal was to view people, places and things in remote time and space in order to gather intelligence information on them.

One operation Morehouse describes was a psychic search for Lieutenant Colonel William Higgins, a United Nations observer who had been taken hostage in Lebanon in 1988. Although Higgins was moved often, the Sun Streak remote viewing team was able to provide information about his whereabouts and his physical and emotional state. To Morehouse's knowledge, no rescue operation was ever launched, which caused great distress to the viewing team. Higgins died at the hands of his kidnappers.

When U.S. hostages were being held and hidden in Iran in 1979–80, a naval officer connected to the National Security Council was working with remote viewers at the Stanford Research Institute in California. The viewers were able to relay their impressions about the hostages' health and location. The viewers regretted that they weren't consulted about the raid to free the hostages. They felt they could have provided helpful information.

In the early 1980s, the U.S. Army Intelligence and Security Command, under the direction of General Albert Stubblebine, used psychics to remotely view the interior of suspected criminal Manuel Noriega's house in Panama. The result was a top-secret two-page report that has remained classified.

During the Gulf War in 1991, Sun Streak remote viewers monitored Iraqi president Saddam Hussein's hide-outs. According to David Morehouse, he and his colleagues were frustrated because they did not know what happened to their information after it was given to their superior officers. They never knew if or when their remote viewing was helpful, and there was never any official acknowledgement of their work.

PSYCHIC SABOTAGE

Often, when competition is fierce and stakes are high, someone will try to sabotage the performance of an enemy or competitor. Some of the best examples of psychic sabotage come from chess competitions. During the 1978 World Chess Championship, Victor Korchnoi accused his opponent, Anatoly Karpov, of using ESP to defeat him. Vladimir Zoukhar was a member of Karpov's training team. According to Korchnoi,

> *Dr. Zoukhar influenced me and forced me to*
> *make mistakes. He bombarded me with negative*
> *suggestions like "You are a traitor to the Soviet*
> *Union, you don't deserve to win, stop playing."*

When Korchnoi conceded the match, he blamed Zoukhar for his defeat. Other chess champions have complained about disruptive psychic energy as well. Boris Spassky and Gary Kasparov say they have felt negative and destructive energy directed towards them during important matches.

MORE PSI SPIES

PSI AGAINST DRUG CRIME

Sun Streak viewers working for the U.S. Army were also called upon to help identify drug smugglers. According to David Morehouse, the former military officer who took part in the program, they advised authorities about which ships were carrying illegal narcotics. They also found sites of planned open-water drops and located buried drug stashes on islands throughout the Caribbean. The American Counter Narcotics Joint Task Force has confirmed that remote viewers have saved the force millions of dollars on search-and-seizure operations.

In 1992 ninety Russian customs officers were trained to use their ESP to locate drugs and other contraband. According to *The European,* more than eighty kilograms of drugs were seized at one checkpoint in one month. The customs chief stated that those officers trained in ESP detected more drugs than other officers.

PSI SPIES IN OUTER SPACE?

NASA (National Aeronautics and Space Administration) officials have reported that psi research is a top priority in the Russian space program. In the 1960s, Chairman Kruschev declared, "We've already used ESP in space!"

According to a 1967 issue of *Soviet Maritime News,* a psi training system has been incorporated into the Russian cosmonaut program. It also reported that cosmonauts, when in orbit, were better able to communicate telepathically with each other than with people on Earth. This could indicate that conditions in outer space actually facilitate ESP. It will take much more research, however, to determine if this is indeed so.

CHAPTER 9

Animal
and Plant ESP

Anyone who has pets knows how sensitive and perceptive they can be. Chuck, who's eighteen, told me about his dog, Rusty:

> *If I just think about taking Rusty for a walk, he runs to the door, all excited. And he knows when I'm going somewhere without him too because he gets depressed and kind of mopes around.*

Animals have such highly developed physical senses that it is not always clear whether ESP is at work or not. For example, rabbits communicate by thumping on the ground with their hind feet. You and I wouldn't hear a thing, but another rabbit could hear a single foot-thump 200 metres away!

Dogs also hear sounds that are not audible to the human ear, and their sense of smell is much more acute than ours. A dog's nose has 220 million cells associated with its sense of smell. (Humans have only 5 million.)

Because they have such sensitive noses, dogs are used by police to smell for bombs. Customs officials routinely use dogs to catch drug smugglers because specially trained dogs can smell drugs that have been sealed in many layers of plastic.

According to *The Canadian Medical Post,* dogs can be trained to smell cancer cells in people. George is a grey-haired Schnauzer who has been trained to detect skin cancer cells in humans. Dr. Armand Gognetta, a skin cancer specialist, says George has a success rate of nearly 100 percent. George was trained after a medical journal described another dog who kept sniffing at a particular mole on her owner's leg, although she ignored all her owner's other moles. A biopsy revealed that the mole was malignant!

Other dogs can warn people suffering from epilepsy that a seizure is coming. Researchers are not sure how dogs can sense oncoming seizures, but they do know that dogs are sensitive to impending epileptic seizures about forty minutes before they actually occur. They can be trained to warn their owners that a seizure is coming so that the owner can take whatever precautions are necessary for safety.

Many animals seem to know when an earthquake is imminent. Caitlin, who lives in California, says,

> *My family boards horses for our neighbours. On*
> *the day of the earthquake, none of the horses*

would let us ride them. They were skittish and
nervous. We tried to ride them in the morning
and couldn't. The earthquake happened late that
same afternoon.

The Chinese government has published an official booklet that describes strange animal signs that precede earthquakes. For example, cattle and horses will not enter corrals, rats come out of hiding and run about wildly and fish jump out of water.

Some animal feats, however, are so incredible that the only plausible explanation seems to be ESP. Nicole told me:

When Daisy, our dog, rushes to the door and
starts to whine and wag her tail, I know my mom
will be home in exactly twenty minutes. If she
works overtime and doesn't get home till 11:30,
Daisy's at the door at 11:10. If Mom gets home
at 6:30, Daisy's at the door at 6:10!

Daisy is not alone in her ability. British biologist Rupert Sheldrake conducted an experiment in which he simultaneously recorded humans at work and their dogs at home. The moment the person left work, the dog at home headed for the door, even if the person left home at a different time each day.

Many pets seem to know in advance that their owner is in danger. Wildlife writer George Laycock tells of a collie whose owner worked in an explosives factory. Each day the collie would walk to work with the man. But one day, while walking to work as usual, the dog began to whine and sat down on the road. The dog wouldn't budge and finally the owner went off to work alone. The collie went home and crawled under the man's bed. He stayed there all morning, whining. That day, a terrible explosion destroyed the factory. The collie's owner was one of the people killed.

Some animals can sense when their owners are ill. Perri says:

> *When I'm not feeling well, Puff, my cat, seems to know it. She will rub against me and purr. She really seems to know when I am down. When I'm feeling good, she's much more independent.*

Naomi, one of my own friends, became seriously ill while away on holiday. She had to be flown by emergency helicopter to the hospital in the middle of the night. Back home, the friend who was taking care of Naomi's two dogs had a sleepless night. The dogs, for no apparent reason, began howling in the middle of the night. Only later did the friend realize that the dogs had begun to howl at the moment Naomi fell ill.

Some animals seem to have the ability to sense when their owners have died. One kennel owner tells of a dog who started howling at 3 a.m. She says,

> *I had never heard the dog make such a terrible racket before. He howled and cried, waking all*

the other animals up. Nothing would comfort
him. All night he howled and none of us got back
to sleep. The next morning, I received news that
the dog's owners had been killed in a car crash.
The accident had happened at 3 a.m!

Writer Ernest Thompson Seton's life was saved by his dog
Bingo. While working by himself in the wilderness, Seton acci-
dently got caught in two wolf traps. By nightfall, a pack of hun-
gry wolves had gathered around him. The leader began to growl
and snap at Seton, who was trapped and helpless. Just as the
wolves were about to attack, Seton's dog Bingo sprang out of the
darkness and killed the leader of the pack. Bingo then managed to
drag over a tool that Seton needed to undo the traps and free himself. After his terrifying ordeal, Seton made his way home. There,
his worried friends told him of Bingo's unusual behaviour while
Seton had been away. Seton recounts it:

The night before, though never taken on the
trapping rounds, the brave dog had acted
strangely, whimpering and watching the timber
trail. At last . . . in spite of attempts to detain
him, he had set out in the gloom and, guided by a
knowledge that is beyond us, reached the spot in
time to avenge me as well as set me free.

Sometimes *people* receive messages that their *pets* are in danger. Oscar Hewitt was an Englishman who lived outside London. While staying with friends he dreamed about his cat Mitzi. In the dream Mitzi was bleeding profusely; one of her ears was nearly torn off. In the morning, the telephone rang. It was Hewitt's housekeeper calling to tell him that Mitzi was badly injured. The cat had come in through his bedroom window in the night and leaped onto his bed, bleeding and crying. One of her ears had been nearly ripped off!

H. Rider Haggard dreamed his dog Bob was lying dead in a clump of weeds near some water. He wrote:

> *The next day Bob was found dead in just such a place. He had been hit by a train at the same time that I'd had my dream.*

There are countless tales of lost or abandoned animals that have travelled thousands of kilometres to find their human families. One of the most famous stories appeared in newspapers throughout Europe during World War I. It was about Prince, an Irish terrier belonging to a man named Jones-Brown. When Jones-Brown enlisted in the army, he left Prince behind with his family in Ireland. Prince became a real problem. He refused to eat, and seemed to become depressed. He was taken on a family trip to England, and promptly disappeared. Mrs. Jones-Brown wrote to her husband to tell him that Prince was gone. Her husband wrote back with unbelievable news: Prince was with him in France! He had somehow managed to cross the English Channel and find his way through various military units until he located his master.

And there is the story of Bobbie, the collie that was lost by his family in Indiana. Six months later he turned up at the family home in Oregon — almost 5000 kilometres away!

ANIMAL PSYCHICS

Animal psychics claim to have a gift for communicating with animals. Some pet owners consult animal psychics when their pets have problems such as carpet wetting or uncontrollable barking.

Raphaela Pope is a full-time animal psychic who lives in California. She has been communicating with animals for more than twenty years. She says that at first, she did readings only for friends and family. Now she is much more serious about it and has begun to advertise to spread the word around. She tells of a woman who lived 400 kilometres away who called to report that her cat had disappeared. Pope was able to locate the cat and relayed the description of boarded-up buildings and parking meters to the owner. When the owner found the only place in her small town that matched this description, she also found her cat.

Sam Louie, another animal psychic, says that most people would be capable of communicating with animals if they could just let go of their skepticism. He says, "This is something everyone is born with. I believe this is something we lose by developing such an emphasis on speech."

ESP AND PLANTS

Like animals, plants have truly incredible sensitivities and abilities. Their fine, threadlike root hairs can detect the direction of the pull of gravity. They can detect water in buried pipes. A root hair the size of a piece of thread can bore through concrete. Plants are able to distinguish between sounds that are inaudible to the human ear. They can distinguish different colour wavelengths such as infrared and ultraviolet that are invisible to the human eye.

They are sensitive to X-rays and to the high frequency of television. Like animals, some plants can warn of impending earthquakes. The Indian licorice plant is so sensitive to electrical and magnetic influences that it is used as a weather plant. Botanists have found that it can predict disturbances such as cyclones, hurricanes, tornadoes, earthquakes and volcanic eruptions.

And, like animals, plants have abilities that seem to indicate that they, too, have ESP.

DAVE THE TELEPATHIC DRACAENA

Dave is a dracaena plant, much like any other dracaena you've ever seen. But Dave happened to belong to Cleve Backster, a leading lie-detector instructor in the United States.

One day Backster was experimenting with his polygraph machine. He attached electrodes to one of Dave's leaves in order to see how the leaf would react to water poured on its roots. When Backster watered Dave, he expected to see increased conductivity as water rose into the plant tissues. But instead, the machine showed a decrease. The galvonometer (a machine that measures electrical current) traced out a pattern that was similar to that of a human being having a pleasant emotional experience.

Backster then wondered how the plant would respond to a threat, and decided to burn it. At his thought, the polygraph pen jumped. Could it be possible that Dave was reading Backster's mind? Backster conducted more experiments that suggested not only that Dave, but other plants as well, had some kind of telepathic ability.

In one amazing experiment, six of Backster's students drew slips of paper out of a hat. One of the slips of paper contained instructions to destroy one of two plants in the room. The "assassin" was to do the deed in secret — neither Backster nor any of the other students would know his identity. Only the surviving plant would be the witness. After the plant had been destroyed, Backster attached the surviving plant to a polygraph and had each student walk by it. The plant gave no reaction to five of the students, but caused the meter to go wild whenever the "assassin" came near.

Some experiments seem to indicate that plants can react in a positive way (by growing quickly, for example) to the positive thoughts and feelings of humans. In one experiment performed in Montreal by Dr. Bernard Grad, plants were given water that had been held in a healer's hands. These grew faster than plants that were given ordinary water.

In Romania, researcher Eugene Celan discovered that plants could mirror the behaviour of other plants. In one of his experiments, Celan added a toxic agent to the water of one plant. A control plant, in a separate container, reacted the same way as the poisoned plant. Celan observed that infection or chemical injury seemed to be communicated to a physically isolated cell. However, this mirror effect was only observed when the cell was isolated in a quartz container. It did not happen when the cell was isolated in a Pyrex container. This could suggest that plant ESP is affected by its environment.

Marcel Vogel, a research scientist with IBM, has devised many experiments that appear to show ESP in plants. He has been able to speed plant growth by thinking positively about them. He also says it is possible to keep cut plants alive longer by thought.

To conduct your own plant ESP experiments at home, just follow these steps:

1) Plant three trays of quick-growing seeds. Be sure to use the same planting soil in each tray.

2) Number each tray.

3) Think and express kind thoughts about tray one. Do not think about tray two at all. Think and express bad and negative thoughts about tray three.

4) Be sure all three trays get the same amount of light and water.

5) After a few days, observe if there are any differences in the trays.

Another experiment you can do is the following: Pick two healthy leaves from a tree or plant. Put one leaf on a saucer and try to ignore it. Put the other leaf on another saucer and think about it at least three times a day. Look at it, praise it, give it positive, loving energy. After a week, compare the two leaves. Is there any difference?

Marlene was able to save a prized hibiscus plant that had frozen after being accidentally left outside overnight. She says:

> *Some friends suggested we try a ritual healing. I figured I had nothing to lose. We formed a circle around my frozen, leafless hibiscus and sang to it. We wished it good health and recovery, and do you know? The plant actually recovered! Of course I can't prove that it was our thoughts that saved my plant, but I believe it was.*

Does your home have a plant that looks dead or dying? Do a good deed and try out your psi. You might save a plant!

CHAPTER 10

Fakes and Frauds

*Oh Louie, Louie, what fools we've been! That was
the most fantastic fraud I ever could imagine!*

These were the first words J. B. Rhine said to his wife Louisa after
leaving a séance given by a famous medium named Margery. (A
medium is someone who goes into a trance state and receives
information from a spirit entity.)

The entire evening had so obviously been a fake that Rhine was
mortified by his gullibility. The world of ESP has always been
plagued with fakes and frauds and Margery the medium was no
exception. Although Rhine was upset that he had been taken for
such a fool, it was this phony séance that inspired him to study
psychic phenomena. He hoped that in carefully controlled laboratory conditions, he could separate cases of genuine ESP from the
frauds who used tricks and scams.

And there have been plenty of scams! In 1848 two Canadian-born sisters began one of the biggest psychic hoaxes on record. Originally from Consecon, near Belleville, Ontario, the Fox family later moved to Hydesville, New York. Kate Fox, who was twelve years old, and her fifteen-year-old sister Margaret became instant celebrities after claiming they could communicate with the spirit of a peddler who had been murdered in their house years before. This communication took place by means of coded rapping sounds that could be clearly heard by witnesses when the girls were present.

Kate and Margaret began to give public performances before astonished audiences. Prominent citizens formed committees to investigate but no explanation could be found. In 1850 the girls toured the United States to packed theatres.

Thirty-eight years later, Margaret Fox confessed that she and her sister had perpetuated a hoax right from the beginning. Before an astonished audience, Margaret took off her shoes, climbed onto a table and demonstrated how she produced the rapping sound by snapping the joint of her big toe!

The *New York Herald* quoted Margaret as saying, "I have been mainly instrumental in perpetuating a fraud . . . it is the greatest sorrow of my life. I began the deception when I was too young to know right from wrong."

In his book *The Psychic Mafia*, Lamar Keene describes the tricks that he and other so-called psychics used to fool people into believing they had genuine ESP. The information that supposedly came through telepathy was actually gathered beforehand and kept on file cards. Sometimes the "psychics" would arrange for a third person to steal or hide an object belonging to a client, and then pretend to "see" its location. The spirits that would appear in séances were actually lengths of gauze and cheesecloth. Keene said he was shocked at how easy it was to fool people.

Many so-called faith healers are actually charlatans who prey on the hopes of the ill and suffering. They plant accomplices in the audience who then pretend to be miraculously cured. Abraham Lincoln knew this and said, "The only person who is a worse liar than a faith healer is his patient!"

Psychics and faith healers have not been the only frauds, however. Some parapsychologists have also cheated in their research. J. B. Rhine discovered that one of his most trusted associates had deliberately changed test scores and falsified records.

PSYCHIC FRAUD-BUSTERS

James Randi, whose stage name is The Amazing Randi, is a professional magician who claims that all psychic phenomena are due to trickery. When he hears of anyone who claims to have psychic abilities, Randi will demonstrate the same abilities by using the tricks and methods that magicians use to fool people.

Uri Geller is one of the psychics that Randi has criticized. Geller began his career as a magician in Israel. His act consists of various mind-reading routines, such as guessing the names of colours or answering questions that are written on a board behind his back. Geller is most famous, however, for his ability to bend metal objects, such as keys and spoons.

Randi has duplicated all of Geller's best-known tricks. He claims that Geller uses an accomplice who signals him from the audience, and that he bends keys physically, not through the power of his mind.

Geller agrees that his feats can be accomplished using stage tricks. But he insists that he uses genuine psychic power, not trickery, in his own act.

Another famous magician who was dedicated to exposing psychic frauds was Harry Houdini. With his friend Joseph Rinn, Houdini unmasked dozens of fraudulent claims of ESP.

Before he died in 1926, Houdini made a pact with his wife. He promised her that, if it were at all possible, he would communicate with her after he died. In order to prevent any kind of fraud, the message would be sent in a secret code known only to Mrs. Houdini. On his deathbed, Houdini is said to have whispered to his wife, "Remember the message . . . When you hear those words . . . know it is Houdini speaking."

For three years, Mrs. Houdini consulted with mediums and other psychics. She never heard the secret code words. But in 1929 the *New York Times* reported that Mrs. Houdini had received the code words at a private sitting with a famous psychic named Arthur Ford.

Mrs. Houdini at first announced to the newspapers that the message was completely genuine. She later withdrew her statement, however, and said she did not believe the message came from her husband after all. Some people thought Mrs. Houdini might have accidentally revealed the code when she was ill, but Arthur Ford swore the message was genuine.

ESP, POWER, AND GREED

Psychic phenomena are big business today. Psychic hotlines alone bring in hundreds of millions of dollars a year in North America. With so much money to be made so easily, many people cannot resist the temptation to cheat.

Donna McCormick, Director of the American Society for Psychical Research, tells of receiving a call from a woman who wanted to know what the going rate was to have a curse lifted. It seems the woman had been to see a psychic who told her that a curse had been put on her. The psychic offered to remove the curse for $5000!

Uri Geller says that although his powers are real, he does sometimes feel the need to cheat. He says that his powers don't always work when he is performing publicly. When this happens, he fakes the trick. But if Geller cheats "some of the time," how is it possible to know when his powers are genuine and when they are not?

Another psychic who has admitted cheating is England's Doris Stokes. She believed she had real powers, but when she first had to perform before a paying audience, she worried that she would dry up and disappoint them. So she cheated. Her spirit guide, however, told her to confess to the audience and she did. Stokes says that she has never cheated since. If nothing comes through for awhile, she accepts it, and doesn't pretend otherwise.

Originally, Greece's Delphic oracle was given offerings, not money, by those who consulted her. Over time, though, the priests became more commercial. As a result, the oracles became a profit-making industry and eventually lost their power. The oracle's last utterance came in A.D. 360, in reply to an inquiry from the emperor Julian:

> Go tell the king: The carven hall is fallen in
>   decay
> Apollo has no chapel left, no prophesizing bay,
> No talking spring. The stream is dry that had so
>   much to say.

When I visited a psychic healer in Bali, I observed him treating a fourteen-year-old girl. Some months earlier, he had correctly diagnosed a brain tumour and sent her for surgery at the hospital. After the operation, the girl was left paralyzed along the right side of her body. The healer was treating her and she had regained nearly all her functioning. He would not accept money from her family. He asked only that they bring him food. He said his gift was from God, and he would lose it if he tried to profit from it.

Edgar Cayce, another gifted psychic, was not tempted by money. People would send him cash and cheques in the mail but he made sure every penny was returned. Cayce was tempted once by power, however. He conducted an experiment in mind control that he later regretted.

He told his assistant that if she named two people, he could will them to come to the photography studio where he worked. The young woman named her brother and another man who was known to dislike Cayce. The next day, the brother came walking down the street. He stood outside the studio for a few minutes and then walked away. But a few minutes later he came back into the studio. His amazed sister asked, "What are you doing here?"

"I don't know," he answered, "But I had some trouble last night at the shop . . . I just wondered if Mr. Cayce could help me out."

The next day, the second man came into the studio. He stood there, looking puzzled, and said "I don't know what I'm doing here. I just came up!" Then he turned and left.

Edgar Cayce never repeated the experiment, saying, "It's one of those things none of us has a right to do . . . anyone who would force another to submit to his will is a tyrant."

BE PSI SMART:
Tricks to watch out for

How can you tell the difference between someone who has genuine ESP and someone who is faking it? Here are some things to watch for in a psychic:

- Overconfidence: If a so-called psychic insists he or she is always "on" or tries to impose one particular vision onto you, watch out!

- Asking for money before the reading: Don't pay for something you have not received.

- Fishing for information: Beware of the psychic who tries to get you to volunteer information. "I see the letter B." You might then say, "Oh, that's Brian, my brother."

- Making general statements: Watch out when a psychic says something that applies to everybody, like, "There is something that you are concerned about."

- Making vague or ambiguous statements: "I see a house in the country, or maybe by the water."

- Using observational skills: Anyone can pick up information about you just by looking at your appearance and your body language. If your hands are calloused, for example, it's not ESP if someone says, "You work with your hands a lot." Or if your shoulders are hunched, it doesn't take ESP to observe you're tense.

- Predicting things that are going to happen anyway: "I see a problem with someone you are close to."

- Giving too much information: This is called the shotgun technique. The so-called psychic speaks quickly and overwhelms you with information, most of it irrelevant. You focus on the bits that have meaning for you, and ignore or forget the rest.

- Careful wording or qualification: "I can see from your hand that you are artistic." If you disagree or somehow show that the psychic is on the wrong track, he then qualifies the statement: "I don't mean you paint or sculpt. I mean you have artistic taste!"

Although these methods may seem obvious, they can be very subtle and effective in practice with a skilled person. As J. B. Rhine learned early in his career, "In psychical research, one dare not take individuals at face value."

As you have seen, believing everything you hear about psi is foolish and could even be dangerous. Although it may be reassuring to believe that a trick is real, it is better to know the hard truth than to believe a comforting fantasy.

CHAPTER • 11

The Real Thing:
Four Famous Psychics

Just about everyone has experienced at least one or two incidents that they would label as ESP. For example, Helen Creighton, the author of *Bluenose Ghosts*, a book about supernatural tales from Nova Scotia, describes one of her own experiences. One day Dr. Creighton was gripped by a strong feeling to cross to the other side of the street, even though that side of the street was more crowded. The urge, though unreasonable, was so strong that Creighton obeyed and crossed the street. At that moment, a street-car stopped in front of her and a friend got off. The woman burst out in relief, "There you are! I've been trying all day to get you on the telephone!" The friend had an urgent message for Creighton.

Most people experience ESP in this way: infrequently and unpredictably. But there are some people whose ESP ability is highly consistent and reliable. One of the most famous and well-documented cases in this category was that of Edgar Cayce.

EDGAR CAYCE:
A genuine psychic

Edgar Cayce was born March 18, 1877, on a farm in Kentucky. One day when he was seven years old, Edgar heard a humming sound and a bright light appeared. As he looked at the light, a figure in white appeared to him. A voice said, "Your prayers have been heard. What would you ask of me, that I may give it to you?" Edgar replied that he wanted only to be helpful to others, especially children who were ill.

The next day, Edgar had a terrible time at school. He misspelled the word cabin and his teacher made him stay after school and write it out 500 times on the blackboard. Then, when Edgar got home, his father gave him more words to spell. Every time Edgar made a mistake, his father would hit him, knocking the little boy right out of his chair. The spelling ordeal continued all evening. By eleven o'clock, Edgar was exhausted. He thought he heard the voice of the previous afternoon say, "Sleep, and we may help you."

He begged his father to let him sleep for just a few minutes. He put his head down on his spelling book and immediately fell asleep. When he woke, he discovered that he could spell every word in the book!

After this incident, Edgar always slept with his schoolbooks under his pillow. But after a few years, this gift faded, and he could no longer take in the contents of a book in this way.

In his early twenties, Cayce lost his voice after a bout of laryngitis. Years of medical treatment did not help. At the suggestion of a hypnotist, Cayce learned to hypnotize himself. When he had put himself into a deep trance, he began to speak in a clear strong voice. He described what was wrong with his throat and described how it should be cured. The remedy worked and Cayce began to help others in the same way.

Throughout his life, Edgar Cayce gave health readings to over 30 000 people. He could describe the physical ailments of total strangers whom he had never seen. All he needed, in order to give a reading, was the person's name and address. Then he would go into a trance and not only describe that person's physical body and ailments, but would also prescribe the appropriate treatment.

While he was in a trance state, Cayce could also give readings in other languages. In all, he spoke twenty-four different languages while in this state. (In his ordinary waking state he could only speak English.)

Even though he could have become a wealthy man, Cayce refused payment for his readings. As a result, he remained poor throughout his life. But he believed that his gift had been given to him by God so that he could help others, and not to profit himself.

When he was asked to explain his remarkable gifts, Cayce replied that his knowledge came from the *patient's* own unconscious mind. He was simply tuning in to the correct frequency: "My experiences have taught me that practically every phase of [psychic] phenomena may be explained by activities of the subconscious mind."

EILEEN GARRETT

Eileen Garrett was born in Ireland in 1893. Orphaned as a baby, she was raised by a kindly uncle and a cold, stern, aunt. She began having clairvoyant experiences when she was four years old. At first she saw visions of children, a boy and two girls. These children looked exactly like human children, except they consisted entirely of light. When Garrett told her aunt about them, she was punished.

Shortly after the children appeared to her, Eileen had another vision. Auntie Leon, her favourite aunt, came to visit, carrying a little baby. Auntie Leon looked tired and ill. She said to Eileen, "I must go away now and take baby with me." Frightened, Eileen ran into the house and told her aunt. When she saw there was no one outside, the aunt gave Eileen a whipping. The next day, the family received the news that Auntie Leon had died while giving birth to her baby!

Eileen Garrett had many more visions, often of people who told her of their impending deaths. During World War I, Garrett married a young soldier. One night while having dinner with some friends, she had a vision of her husband being killed in an explosion. She became ill and went home. A few days later, she learned that her husband was reported missing. He had been sent on a mission the same day of her vision, and he never returned.

In 1930 Garrett astounded even the most skeptical critics. During a psychic reading in England, she was suddenly interrupted by the presence of a spirit that identified itself as Irwin or Irving. The day before, news had reached London of the crash in

France of an experimental airship. Irwin claimed he was that airship's captain. He proceeded to describe the crash in very specific and technical detail.

An official inquiry into the case determined that every one of Garrett's details, as relayed by the presence called Irwin, was correct. One of these details was the phrase uttered by Irwin, "This exorbitant scheme of carbon and hydrogen is entirely wrong." In fact, the model of carbon and hydrogen happened to be a closely guarded official secret. It was an experiment for a new fuel source. Its disclosure by Garrett caused considerable official embarrassment. There were even accusations of "treason by telepathy!"

Later on, Garrett travelled to the United States, where she became the respected president of the Parapsychology Foundation. Her psychic abilities were tested by many serious researchers, including J. B. Rhine and Canada's Humphrey Osmond. The author Aldous Huxley described Eileen Garrett as a gifted and sensitive investigator of psychical research.

Of her own ability, Garrett said, "I had the good fortune to enter it at an early age, when the mind, not too far removed from the mystery of birth, was able to accept wider dimensions in time and space . . . What might be regarded as alien and dangerous by the adult world had no power to inflict doubt on the mind of the child."

In her psychic readings, Garrett received information through a control. She never believed, though, that her controls were independent intelligences. Instead, she thought they were symbols, creations or projections of some level of her own being.

Eileen Garrett became one of the greatest psychics of the twentieth century. For more than fifty years she participated in tests and experiments of all kinds. In spite of her amazing ability, Garrett remained dubious about her talents. She once said, "There may be nothing in it. Nothing at all. Who knows?"

OSKAR ESTEBANY

Oskar Estebany was born in Hungary. He loved horses and eventually became a colonel in a Hungarian cavalry unit. One day his horse became very ill, and Estebany knew the animal would be shot if it did not recover. He stayed with his horse all night in the stable, massaging and stroking it. By morning his horse was well again. In time he discovered that he could heal other animals as well, but never attempted to use his healing ability with humans. One day, however, a neighbour's child became very ill and no doctor was available. In desperation, the child's father brought the youngster to Estebany's house and asked Oskar to heal him in the same way he healed horses. Estebany reluctantly agreed to treat the child, who recovered. He was then persuaded to use his gift to help people. By the time he left Hungary and came to Canada, Estebany was well-known as a psychic healer.

When he moved to Montreal, Estebany began working as a cleaner in a hospital. It was there that he came to the attention of Dr. Bernard Grad, who was conducting research at McGill University. Estebany agreed to participate in scientific studies of his ability. He was curious about how his ability worked, and he submitted patiently to a long list of extensive and demanding tests.

According to Estebany, by placing his hands on or near the site of the disease, he could detect the presence of disease in the person's body. The sensations in his hands would change. He might feel heat or burning, for example. Sometimes he would feel cold, or a tingling or prickling sensation. He said the energy flow increased when he worked with a group of sick people.

Oskar Estebany participated in many other well-controlled experiments. He was able to inhibit the growth of goitres in mice and increase the growth rate of rats and yeast, and his touch speeded the healing of infections in rats and mice.

When asked to explain his powers, Estebany replied, "There is an energy all around us; I just draw on it."

Oskar Estebany lived in Montreal until his death at the age of ninety.

VANGA DIMITROVA

Vanga Dimitrova was a blind Bulgarian clairvoyant. She found missing people, helped solve crimes, diagnosed disease and predicted the future. She was intensively tested by more than thirty scientists, as well as a special government commission. After receiving official government approval, she became a state-employed psychic with two secretaries.

When she was thirteen, Dimitrova began to have bouts of blindness. At the age of nineteen, after two unsuccessful operations, she went completely blind. Shortly after, Dimitrova confided to her family that she "just knew" her father would die soon. Her father did die, on the exact day she had predicted. After that, it was said that she had exchanged one kind of sight for another.

People began coming to Dimitrova from neighbouring villages. When word of her amazing psychic abilities spread, she became famous throughout the whole country. Dimitrova's information was not vague and general — it was specific and detailed.

For example, she told one man who was searching for his brother that the brother was alive but that he was in a German concentration camp. She said the brother had grown up in Russia, and was now a scientist. Dimitrova then told the man that his brother would be released and come to him in the early spring, wearing a grey uniform and carrying two suitcases. The man could not believe all this and was convinced he'd never find out what had happened to his brother.

Two months later, in the early spring, a stranger stopped at the man's house. He was wearing a grey uniform and carrying two suitcases. Twenty years earlier he had run away to Russia. He had gone to school and become a scientist. When the war came, he was captured by the Germans and put into a camp. He managed to convince the Germans that he was Bulgarian, not Russian, and so won his release. Walking, he found his way back to his childhood home!

Dimitrova was not always right. Some days her psychic power didn't come. But, according to the more than thirty scientists who studied her, Dimitrova was right an amazing eighty percent of the time.

People flocked to see Dimitrova. She was becoming exhausted and ill, giving up to fifty readings a day. The government then founded The Institute of Suggestology and Parapsychology, which set up a committee to schedule appointments for her. The institute staff were able to interview those who saw her, as well as research and document her readings.

Dimitrova claimed she had no control over the mental images that formed in her mind. She couldn't force them, and she was often made unhappy by what she saw in her readings. Her sadness was balanced, though, by the comfort she felt when she was able to help people find a missing relative or help the police solve a crime.

Over a million people consulted Dimitrova, including the former king of Bulgaria. Dimitrova died in 1996, at the age of eighty-four.

CHAPTER 12

Apply Your PSI

ESP powers are used in all kinds of interesting ways. Some people, like dowsers, make their living from ESP. Others use ESP as a diagnostic tool by reading auras, or energy fields. Some scholars have even used their ESP to find buried archaeological sites. Here are three different ways you can apply your psi. They are fun to try, and with practice, you might become an expert too!

AURAS

Did you know that there is light radiating from your body? All living things give off energy in some way. There is an electromagnetic field around your body that you can learn to feel and even see. This energy field is called an aura. Some healers can diagnose illness just by assessing a person's aura. Edgar Cayce said, "Ever since I can remember I have seen colours in connection with people . . . blues and greens and reds gently pouring from their heads and shoulders. It was a long time before I realized that other people did not see these colours. Sickness, dejection, love, fulfillment — these are all reflected in the aura, and for me the aura is the weather vane of the soul."

Many scholars think that the halos in paintings of angels, saints and other religious or spiritual figures were the artists' attempts to show a strong energy or aura.

There is a special kind of photographic technique called Kirlian photography, in which you can take a picture of a person's electromagnetic field. Kate had her aura photographed this way: She had to put on a black cloak that covered her body and put her hand on a metal plate that was hooked up to a special camera. She says:

I didn't feel anything, it was just like having an
ordinary picture taken. But when the film was
developed, there were red waves swooping around
my head! There was a big red ball on my chest,
around my heart. My friend had hers done too,
and her aura was totally different. She had
different layers of yellow, green, blue and violet.
It was really beautiful!

To practise seeing your aura, make sure the room you are in is dimly lit. If the light is too bright or too dark, you won't be able to see your aura. Also, be careful not to look directly into the light. Begin by feeling the "empty" space between your two hands. Hold them in front of you, palms facing but not touching. Slowly move your hands away from each other, until they are about fifteen centimetres apart. Then move them close together again, and then apart. Keep your motions slow and steady. Repeat this a few times. Can you feel something building up between your hands? What does it feel like?

Now, take your hands farther apart, about twenty to twenty-five centimetres. Slowly bring them back together until you feel a pressure pushing your hands out. It should feel just a litle harder to bring your hands together. When you feel that slight resistance, you are feeling your body's energy field.

Some people feel a warmth or tingling when they try this. Others feel a pulsing sensation. Take a moment and be aware of what *you* are feeling in your hands – it might be something quite different. When you can feel your energy field, you are ready to try seeing it.

In front of a plain wall, stretch your arm out and look at your hand. Soften your gaze by letting your eyes go a little out of focus, or try squinting them. Don't be afraid to experiment.

Relax your body and look at the outline of your hand. Now look at the space about a centimetre away from your hand. Spread your fingers out and then close them. Do you see anything around your hand? Now slowly move your other hand out in front of you. Move your hands up and down, bring them close together and move them apart. Move your hands so that different fingers are pointing to each other. Do you see anything? When you can see a faint haze of light or colour, that's it – you're seeing your aura! Soon you can practise seeing auras on other people. In time, you might be able to see colours as well!

When you can see your own aura, there are some other things you can look for. Is the outline smooth or jagged? Are there holes or breaks in it? This could indicate a problem or illness. Is the aura strong and vibrant or thin and patchy? Are there several colours or just one? Do the colours change? If they change, does your mood change as well?

DOWSING

Dowsers are people who can find water or minerals under the ground. They do this by walking over a chosen site holding sticks or rods. In the past, dowsers used hazel or willow twigs that were cut into the shape of the letter Y, although any kind of stick can be used. The Bible records that Moses once found water with his staff. Some dowsers use only their bare hands and are called hand tremblers. Today, many dowsers use metal L-shaped rods or pendulums. The rod will twist or bend down when water is directly underneath. If the dowser uses a pendulum, it will twirl over the water.

Keith did some dowsing at camp. He told me:

> We used forked sticks. I felt sort of stupid at first, walking around and holding a stick out in front of me. But I came to one place and I swear the stick nearly jumped out of my hands! It was like there was a force pulling it from underneath the ground. Later on, I discovered there was an underground well where my stick had jumped.

121

Mining companies employ dowsers to find minerals such as gold and copper. Some electrical companies use dowsers to locate underground power cable failures. Every major pipeline company in North America has a dowser on its payroll.

U.S. Marines used dowsers in Vietnam to find hidden land mines and underground tunnels. Sometimes their dowsing rods were made from coat hangers.

Dowsers can often find water where geological experts cannot. They can provide accurate information about depth, yield and purity.

The pharmaceutical company Hoffman-LaRoche always commissions dowsing surveys when setting up new factories all over the world. Their spokesperson explains: "We use methods that are profitable, whether they are scientifically explainable or not. The dowsing method pays off."

MAKE YOUR OWN DOWSING RODS

Most dowsers today use metal rods or pendulums when they dowse. You can easily make your own instruments. To make dowsing rods, take two wire coat hangers. Cut the hangers at A and B, as shown. (If you use wire cutters, you might need an adult's help.) Straighten out the two hangers so that the sides form ninety-degree angles.

To make holders for the rods, you will need two tubes of cardboard, each about ten centimetres long. You could also glue two empty thread spools together. Insert the hangers into the tubes or spools, as shown.

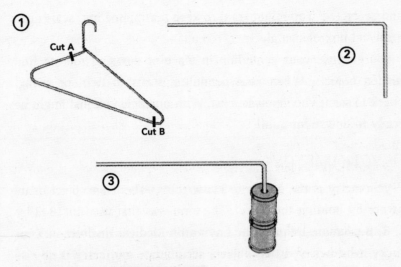

DOWSING EXPERIMENT

Ask a friend to place three identical pieces of paper on the floor and to hide a coin under one of them. Hold your divining rods with their long arms parallel to the floor, pointing out in front of you. Now begin to walk around the room, passing your rods over each piece of paper. Take your time. Try to keep your mind relaxed and open. If the rods swing together and cross over, or pull downward as you pass over the hidden coin, you've made a hit!

You can also dowse with a pendulum, if you prefer. To make a pendulum, take a length of string about thirty centimetres long, and tie a small object to the end of it. The object should be heavy enough so the string will hang straight down, but not so heavy that it won't swing easily. A ring or a crystal or small stone will work well. When you are not using your pendulum, keep it safe and protected. You might want to keep it wrapped in a scarf or in a special box or container.

You can use your pendulum in place of dowsing rods to find hidden objects. When your pendulum starts to twirl or swing, check to see if you've made a hit. With practice, you just might be ready to dowse for gold!

PSYCHOMETRY

Psychometry is the ability to know things about an object or its owner by holding the object. The term was first used in 1843 by J. R. Buchanan, Dean of the Covington Medical Institute in Kentucky, who believed that objects accumulate and carry their histories with them.

Dr. Buchanan's experiments showed that some of his students could detect different chemicals wrapped in thick brown paper. Some of them could also hold unopened letters in their hands and describe the people who had written them.

Another teacher, geologist William Denton, tested his students with rock samples. He found that some of them could describe, with amazing accuracy, the origin of the samples.

Buchanan concluded that all materials give off emanations that are affected by human emotion. He believed that the world's history is recorded on objects. This information can be picked up and decoded by "sensitives." He regarded psychometry as no more remarkable than the power to hear or see.

In 1926 the famous mystery writer Agatha Christie suddenly disappeared, setting off a national search in England. The police had found Christie's abandoned car on the edge of a chalk pit with its motor still running — foul play was suspected. Sir Arthur Conan Doyle, the creator of Sherlock Holmes, called in a psychometrist to assist in the investigation. Conan Doyle gave him one of Christie's gloves and later recounted:

> *I gave him no clue at all as to what I wanted or*
> *to whom the article belonged. He never saw it*
> *until I laid it on the table, and there was nothing*
> *to connect either it or me with the Christie case.*
> *He at once got the name of Agatha. "There is*
> *trouble connected with this article. The person*
> *who owns it is half dazed and half purposeful.*
> *She is not dead as many think. She is alive.*
> *You will hear of her, I think, next Wednesday."*

Agatha Christie was found the next Tuesday night, but it was not until Wednesday morning that the news was released. She was registered at a hotel in northern England, under another name. She was suffering from amnesia, brought on by a crisis in her life.

There are so many recorded examples of information obtained by psychometry that it is considered to be one of the most common and easily accessible forms of ESP available.

A doctor told me this story:

> *Once a new patient told me he had psychic*
> *powers. I guess I looked skeptical because he*

offered to prove it. He asked me to let him hold
something that belonged to me, something
personal. I gave him my wallet. He held it and
described the inside of my house in great detail
. . . Then he said, "Uh oh, I'd better stop here.
I'm starting to learn too much. If you're going to
be my doctor, I don't want to know about your
personal problems!"

To try psychometry yourself, take several small objects that have
some history or meaning to you, such as a piece of jewellery, a
key, a scarf or an old coin. A small object that belonged to a par-
ent or grandparent is excellent. Spend a few minutes holding and
looking at each article. Then hold each piece to your forehead. Let
mental images come to you. Don't censor the thoughts and images
that come.

Now repeat this experiment with a friend. Ask your friend to
select three objects which have some kind of history or story
attached to them, and let your friend have three objects that
belong to you. Hold and look at the pieces. Do you feel any energy coming from them? Now hold each object to your forehead
and, as before, let thoughts, feelings and images come to you.
Exchange these impressions with your friend. Did either of you
pick up information or history about the articles?

Repeat this experiment with different objects. If you like, you
can disguise the objects by wrapping them or placing them in
containers. Some psychometrists do this so the appearance of the

article won't give them any clues as to its history.

If you don't succeed at first, don't give up. This ability nearly always improves with practice!

CHAPTER 13

Develop Your ESP Potential

You can develop your ESP ability by increasing your awareness of yourself, other people and the world around you. Karl Nikolaiev, a Russian psychic, says: "I chose to become telepathic. I did not have any unusual experiences or talents as a child. I worked hard to realize potential most people don't even think about. I trained myself to be psychic."

People with highly developed mental, physical or spiritual abilities agree that they were able to develop their abilities by study and practice.

SENSITIVITY AND PRACTICE

Psychic ability depends on heightened senses, both inner and outer. The more sensitive you are, the more likely you are to be aware of psychic experiences. In the past, men and women who had ESP were called "sensitives."

128

People who train their senses can develop amazing powers. For example, some wine tasters can tell you on which side of a hill the grapes grew and in what kind of soil! These people weren't born with exceptional sensitivity. They developed their senses by concentration and practice. Charles Bourdon, a famous French perfume maker says: "Everyone has an average nose. It's training that makes a good one. You have to concentrate on the smells. Then you start to smell well and you can focus on each detail among all the ingredients in a fragrance."

The same principle applies to developing ESP. Noreen Renier, a psychic who works with police, believes that "You have to practise continually. It has to be part of your life. I try to show people I'm not something special. This ability is not something to fear. It's something we all have that with work, with practice, we can develop."

ATTITUDE IS IMPORTANT

It's OK to have fun! An adventurous and playful approach is more helpful than a serious, self-conscious attitude. You will be more receptive and aware if you are relaxed and at ease than if you are tense and focused on "doing it right." In fact, forget all about doing it right. What you want to discover is how *you* do it. However you experience ESP is the right way for you.

VALUE YOUR INTUITION

Intuition is the foundation of all ESP experiences, and some psychics prefer to call themselves intuitives. Intuition is the ability to know something without going through the usual cognitive or reasoning process. It's when you know something without knowing why or how you know it. You will find that the more you actually listen to what your intuition is telling you and then act on it, the stronger it will become. Craig says,

> *My intuition is not right 100 percent of the time*
> *but it is right most of the time. The few times it*
> *has been wrong are way overshadowed by the*
> *millions of times it's been right. And the more I*
> *listen to it, the righter it gets!*

Ignored intuition will wither and disappear. Instead of ignoring what your intuition tells you, begin to listen to it. Think about it. Have there been times when you didn't listen to your intuition and you wished that you had?

Godfrey Mowat, a blind healer, ignored his own awakening psychic ability and regretted it. When he was a young man in his early twenties, he awoke one night and heard a voice telling him to warn a guest who was staying at his family's home. He said:

> *I must admit I was too scared of being laughed at*
> *to say anything to her at first. But the next night*
> *I heard the same thing again and this time I was*
> *more frightened of not telling her than of being*
> *ridiculed. Strangely enough, as soon as I told her,*

she went home. She found her brother lying
across the dining table — he had shot himself.
Had I warned the girl that first night, she might
have had time to save his life. I made a vow that
in future I would disregard all doubt.

Even the U.S. Air Force, in an officers' training booklet, confirms the value of intuition in decision-making. It refers to a study that advises officers to "be aware that your hunches can be valuable and be alert so that you can recognize your own ESP when it occurs."

Many psychics believe that their ESP comes from their ability to easily switch into a right-brain mode. According to current biological theories, the right hemisphere of the brain is the seat of creativity and intuition — it's the artistic side. The left hemisphere is the seat of analytical thinking — the scientific side. Psychic Noreen Renier contends that "psychics aren't analytical or organized. We're into this emotional, intuitive side."

Acting on your feelings of intuition is the bridge that can make ESP experiences available to you.

KNOW HOW YOUR BODY RESPONDS TO PSYCHIC ENERGY

Not everybody picks up ESP in the same way. Some people see images and others might hear voices or feel body sensations, such as the woman in the following story. This case was substantiated by both the woman's doctor and hospital staff:

> *I went to see my doctor, because for about thirty minutes this morning I felt as though every bone in my body was broken. The doctor examined me, but found nothing wrong. When I returned home, I received a phone call from the hospital. I was told that my brother had been brought into the hospital after running his car off a cliff. He had only lived for thirty minutes, and it appeared as if every bone in his body was broken.*

Another man, Darcy, picks up ESP in another way. There are people and things that literally leave him with a bad taste in his mouth. Darcy once had a dream that had no images or story. He just dreamed he was smelling and tasting smoke. He woke up with such a strong taste and smell of smoke that he got up and checked if his apartment was really on fire. The next day he received a phone call from his mother. Her house had caught fire during the night.

Catherine is a university student who is studying parapsychology. She told me about a lesson that surprised her:

> *The class sat in a circle and the professor told one student, Mary, to keep her eyes open. The rest of us closed our eyes. Mary was to pick someone from the circle, and to stare at them. Whoever felt they were the one being stared at had to say so before they opened their eyes. I'd never done anything like this before, and I really*

didn't know what to expect. In a minute or two,
I began to feel this warm glow in my stomach.
I ignored it, because I thought if Mary were
looking at me, I'd sense something on my face.
But the warmth in my stomach didn't go away.
It got hotter and hotter. Then, without even
knowing I was going to say anything, I just
started to laugh, and I said "It's me, I can feel
it's me!" And it was!

Catherine then went on to say that she has learned that it's her stomach that is her ESP responder. She doesn't get images or hear voices. She gets sensations in her stomach.

Ingrid also feels ESP in her body. She says:

I met this really good-looking guy. He was so
cool, but my stomach felt nauseous, which I
ignored, of course, because he was so cute. In
spite of how I felt, I went to his house, and he
assaulted me. It was a hard lesson to learn, but
now I never ignore what my body is feeling.

What are the ways that you experience ESP? Lainie has words that seem to pop into her head from nowhere. Some people have vague feelings of nervousness or unease. Some see actual images or visions.

Others, like the actor Leonardo DiCaprio, feel a tingling somewhere in their bodies. When Leonardo's grandfather had to have his foot amputated, Leonardo says he felt a cold, tingling sensation in his own foot, even though he was hundreds of kilometres away at the time, filming in France.

The writer Michael Crichton tells of a psychic he met who told him that she saw snakes, lots of black snakes, coiled up in some kind of flat baskets. At the time, Crichton was working on the movie *The Great Train Robbery*. He thinks the snakes she saw were the canisters of film that were piled up in his editing room and weighing heavily on his mind.

It's important to know how *you* respond to psi, otherwise you might ignore psychic information that comes to you. Also you might confuse psychic information with your own feelings. For example, if you tend to pick up information in your body and you feel sick or empty, you might think there is something wrong with you. It could be useful to ask yourself, "What am I in conflict about? What is my body telling me about this person or situation? What do I think or feel at a deeper level in myself?"

Sylvia Choquette, author of *The Psychic Pathway*, described her early childhood awareness of vibrations, or vibes: "Life without vibes would be like being blind or deaf. It was my primary sense, my primary way of experiencing life around me."

It wasn't until later on, in her teens, that Choquette began to see images. She discovered that when she held an object, visions would come to her. She could see, feel and sometimes hear future events. As she studied and practised, Choquette was able to improve and develop her psychic abilities even further.

SENDERS AND RECEIVERS

A good sender is just as important as a sensitive receiver. If the sender's thoughts are hazy and unfocused, the receiver cannot get a clear message or impression. The famous psychic Wolf Messing once said: "How clearly a thought comes through depends on the ability of the sender to concentrate. If a crowd of conflicting thoughts streams through the sender's mind, my own impressions will blur."

Some people are better at sending information than receiving it. Here's an interesting experiment you can try with a friend to discover if you are better at sending or receiving:

Before the experiment, decide which of you will be the sender. The sender then selects four pictures from old magazines. Almost any kind of picture will do: drawings, paintings, cartoons or photographs. Cut out the pictures and put them into four identical envelopes. The sender then sits in another room, shuffles the four envelopes and selects one. After opening the envelope he or she should sit quietly and comfortably and concentrate on the picture for about fifteen minutes.

In the other room, the receiver relaxes and stays aware of any images, sensations and impressions that occur. When the time is up, the receiver draws a sketch of any shapes or colours that come to mind. The sender says nothing at all and keeps the chosen picture a secret during this time. The receiver does all the talking for about five minutes, mentioning impressions or sensations that stand out. Then the sender takes the four pictures out of their envelopes and the receiver chooses the one he or she thinks it is.

Switch roles with your friend and repeat the experiment using four new pictures. Did you do better as a sender or a receiver?

LEARN TO MEDITATE

Meditation is the act of relaxing, calming and focusing your mind and body. A relaxed state of mind will increase ESP ability. A French psychologist named Pierre Janet taught one of his patients to meditate. When she was in a deep, meditative state, he asked her to see what his friend Charles Richet, who later won the Nobel Prize for medicine, was doing in Paris. (Janet was in Le Havre, 190 kilometres away.) The woman began to shout, "It's burning, I tell you it's burning!" She then went on to describe how a fire was raging in Richet's laboratory. Richet verified her description of this fire, which had destroyed his laboratory at the same time the patient "saw" it.

If you can set aside only ten or fifteen minutes a day for meditation, you will be rewarded with increased powers of concentration and greater ESP ability. You will also feel more relaxed and less stressed-out. There are many ways to meditate. The aim of all meditative techniques is to clear away the distractions and chatter of the mind. Some people repeat a phrase such as "I am relaxed and aware." Some people focus on a word or image. Some chant or pray. What's important is to find the technique that works for you and to practise it regularly. Meditation works best if you do it for a short time, about fifteen minutes or so, every single day. Here are two simple meditations you can try.

TREE MEDITATION

Choose a tree that appeals to you and sit comfortably in a quiet place. In a relaxed, casual way, gaze at the tree. Look at its overall shape and size. Become aware of its specific qualities: its trunk, branches and leaves. What is the colour and texture of its bark? Watch how it moves in the wind. If your mind starts to wander, simply bring it back to focus on the tree. Continue to gaze at the tree for fifteen minutes. Let go of any expectations about what may or may not happen. Most people have a different experience each time they meditate. Try it and see what happens for you.

BREATH MEDITATION

Sit in a comfortable position in a quiet room. Close your eyes and become aware of your breathing. Take in a slow, deep breath and then exhale fully. Now, as you inhale, count slowly to four. Hold your breath and count to four, and exhale, again counting to four. If your mind begins to wander, gently bring it back to the awareness and counting of your breathing.

Whichever way you choose to meditate, you may sometimes have difficulties. You may feel restless and fidgety, your mind may wander. This is normal. Just keep at it and you will become calmer, more observant and more open to different levels of awareness. Through meditation, you slowly learn to focus your awareness inward, making you receptive to deeper levels of information and knowledge that are available to you.

KEEP A JOURNAL

Write down your intuitions, your hunches, your dreams. Make note in your journal of body sensations, phrases or words that pop into your head out of nowhere. Record any strange, coincidental or odd events. These things have been happening all along. By keeping a journal, you are raising your awareness of them.

And don't be afraid to check out your hunches. Ray told me that when he first started writing down his predictions about things, he was discouraged because nothing ever seemed to come true. But one time he had a strong feeling that his buddy Cal was going to visit him on a Friday night. Well, Cal didn't come that night, but he did come the following Friday. When Ray told him that he'd had a feeling that Cal might come the week before, he was amazed when Cal told him that he'd tried to come then. He'd actually loaded up his car and started out but had to turn back because of car trouble!

As you develop deeper powers of awareness and concentration, you will begin to see patterns to things that at first seemed random and coincidental.

WHAT'S YOUR VERDICT?

Are you a sheep or a goat? A believer or non-believer in ESP? Or do you remain decidedly undecided?

Whatever your conclusions about ESP, I hope these true stories of the human mind have conveyed to you some of the wonder and awe I felt as I was writing about them.

In Chapter 3, How Does ESP Work?, Dr. Humphrey Osmond

beautifully described a kind of invisible web that runs through everything. But just like a spider's web, these connections are fragile and often difficult to see. Thankfully, science is helping us to see these fine, fragile strands that link all things together. Our scientists are constantly discovering ever-deepening levels of meaning and connection between all creatures, all people and all life.

I was saddened, as perhaps you were, when I learned how much time, money and effort governments have spent in their attempts to use psychic ability as a weapon for war. If only these same efforts could be put into exploring how ESP could be used as a tool for greater understanding and healing in the world, then we might not need weapons of any kind!

Nonetheless, as we become more aware, we will see more of what was previously invisible. And most of the potential and power of our minds remains invisible to us. As Thomas Edison so rightly said, "We do not know one-millionth of one percent about anything."

The power of the human mind is vast. The possibilities for life, discovery and creativity are endless. We owe it to ourselves, and to each other, to nurture and protect this amazing gift.

What about you? How will you use your own boundless, wild and wonderful psi?

GLOSSARY OF PSYCHIC TERMS

AGENT: The "sender" in tests for telepathy. Also, the person who looks at the target object in ESP tests.

AURA: The energy field that emanates from all living things.

AUTOMATIC WRITING: Writing or drawing that is channelled through a medium while in a trance state. Afterwards, the medium has no memory or understanding of the information that was produced. Some people have channelled music they believe was dictated to them by great composers such as Beethoven and Brahms.

CALL: The subject's guess or response in trying to identify the target in an ESP test.

CHANNELLING: Receiving information from a soul or spirit guide. The "channeller" becomes the mouthpiece of an "entity." Often the channeller will speak in a different voice than usual. He or she may also speak in a different accent or use very old-fashioned language.

CLAIRAUDIENCE: "Clear hearing," the ability to hear sounds that are not audible to others, especially calls of distress from a loved one.

CLAIRVOYANCE: "Clear seeing," the ability to see or know things, usually in the form of visions or mental "impressions."

CONTROL: The personality, often experienced as a spirit or entity, who acts as a guide for a medium in a trance. Some mediums believe their controls are the spirits of people who have died. Others believe they are split-off parts of the medium's own personality.

CRISIS APPARITION: The appearance, usually to a loved one, of a person either dying or under great stress.

DIVINATION: Any system for enquiring into hidden matters by means other than the five senses. For example, tarot cards and crystal gazing are ways of divining. In ancient times, diviners examined animal entrails to foretell the future.

DOWSING: The ability to find hidden or buried objects and energy sources, such as water or minerals, using sticks, rods or pendulums. Some dowsers, called "hand tremblers," use only their bare hands.

ESP: Extrasensory perception, the ability to pick up information by means other than the five senses.

FORTUNETELLING: The ability to know or predict events that have not yet occurred. Fortunetellers often use a form of divination to focus on during a reading.

GANZFELD: A German word meaning uniform field. ESP tests which are conducted while the subject is in a state of sensory deprivation.

INTUITION: Knowing something without going through any cognitive processing.

KIRLIAN PHOTOGRAPHY: A photographic process that can record the energy field of living things.

MEDIUM: A person, usually in trance, who channels information from other beings.

ORACLE: A person, usually considered holy or spiritual, who could give prophetic advice. Often, the oracle's prophecy is ambiguous and difficult to interpret.

PARANORMAL: Phenomena of a non-physical nature that science cannot yet explain or measure.

PARAPSYCHOLOGY: The branch of science that deals with psychic phenomena.

PK: Another term for psychokinesis.

PRECOGNITION: The prediction of future events which cannot be inferred from present knowledge.

PSI: A general term used to identify different aspects of ESP.

PSYCHIC: A person who has highly developed ESP. Also, a general term used to describe mental, subconscious or spiritual matters.

PSYCHIC ARCHAEOLOGY: The discovery of archaelogical sites through paranormal means such as dowsing, psychometry or clairvoyance.

PSYCHIC SURGERY: Surgery that is performed by healers in a trance state, without medical training or facilities. Also, removing diseased parts of the body without incision.

PSYCHOKINESIS: Influencing the movement of objects using only the mind.

PSYCHOMETRY: The ability to know the history of an object or its owner by holding the object.

REMOTE VIEWING: A technique in which a trained "viewer" tries to see or experience an event that is happening at a distance.

SCRYING: A form of divination that involves staring at a shiny or polished surface to induce a vision or trance state.

SÉANCE: Literally means "sitting down"; refers to the assembly of several people for the purpose of spirit communication or psychic development.

SECOND SIGHT: An old term used to describe psychic ability.

SPONTANEOUS PSI EXPERIENCE: A natural, unplanned occurrence of an event or experience that seems to involve parapsychical ability.

SUBJECT: The person tested in an experiment.

TARGET: The objectives or events a subject tries to discern in ESP experiments.

TELEKINESIS: Another term for psychokinesis or PK.

TELEPATHY: The transfer of information from one person to another using only the mind.

TRANCE: An altered state of consciousness in which a person has access to mental abilities he or she cannot perform in a normal, waking state.

VISION: An object or event not visible to the eye at the place and time it occurs.

ZENER CARDS: A set of five easily visualized symbols used in ESP experiments. Named after their inventor, a Swiss psychologist.

SANDRA COLLIER

Sandra Collier was born in England and moved to Canada as a child. A psychotherapist specializing in dreams, she has lectured extensively and made numerous media appearances. These days her pursuits also include writing short stories, non-fiction and poetry. She is a mother and grandmother who enjoys travelling, gardening and yoga. Sandra's first book was the best-selling *Wake Up to Your Dreams*. She lives in Toronto with her husband.